DINO-TREKKING

DINO-TREKKING

THE ULTIMATE DINOSAUR LOVER'S TRAVEL GUIDE

Kelly Milner Halls

Illustrations by Rick Spears

John Wiley & Sons, Inc.
New York • Chichester • Brisbane • Toronto • Singapore

Copyright © 1996 by Kelly Milner Halls

Published by John Wiley & Sons, Inc.

Illustrations © 1996 by R. C. Spears

Library of Congress Cataloging-in-Publication Data

Halls, Kelly Milner

    Dino-trekking : the ultimate dinosaur lover's travel guide /
Kelly Milner Halls
      p.   cm.
    Includes index.
    ISBN 0–471–11498–7 (acid-free)
    1. Dinosaurs.   2. Dinosaurs—United States—Guidebooks.
  3. Dinosaur paraphernalia—United States—Directories.
  4. Dinosaurs—Collectibles—United States—Directories. I. Title
QE862.D5H224   1996
567.9'1'0973—dc20   95–7877

This book is dedicated to my sweet daughters, Kerry and Vanessa, who knew their mom was a dinosaur long before she got lost on the dinosaur trail.

And to God, for giving us minds that wonder and so much to wonder about!

ACKNOWLEDGMENTS

My heartfelt thanks to the supremely talented Rick Spears for illustrating the Dino-Identifier guide to prehistoric creatures with brilliance and attention to accuracy—and for being my very best friend and "Dino-Pal" in the whole universe. You are the best!

Special thanks to my agent, Al Zuckerman, for taking on a "no name," and to Don Lessem (the definitive dinosaur writer), Dr. Peter Dodson, and RayAnn Havasy at the Dinosaur Society for helping guarantee a high level of excellence and accuracy in this and my other dinosaurian projects.

Though I graciously thank the hundreds of staff members and experts from all locations listed in the book, I must express special appreciation to those who contributed their expertise and wrote "Curator's Corner" entries:

Dr. W. A. Akersten, Idaho State Museum

Mr. Ralph Beane, Nevada, Iowa (Thanks for the lovely crinoid.)

Ms. Brenda Bechter, Museum of Western Colorado

Ms. Rachel Benton, Fossil Butte Monument, Wyoming

Mr. and Mrs. John Brandvold, Montana

Dr. Michael Brett-Surman, National Museum of Natural History

Dr. Peter Crane, Field Museum of Natural History

Mr. Ted Daeschler, Academy of Natural Science, Pennsylvania

Ms. Eleanor Daly, Mississippi Museum of Natural Science

Dr. James P. Diffily, Fort Worth Museum of Science and History

Ms. Kristin Donnan, South Dakota–based freelance writer
    (one *great* gal-pal!)

Dr. James O. Farlow, Purdue University at Fort Wayne

Dr. Nicholas C. Fraser, Virginia Museum of Natural History

Dr. Roland Gangloff, University of Alaska

Dr. David Gillette, Utah State Paleontologist

Dr. Russ Graham, Mastodon State Park

Mr. John Gurche, Denver Museum of Natural History (for inspiration!)

Dr. John R. Horner, Museum of the Rockies, Montana

Mr. Gary Hoyle, Maine State Museum (for helping me see beyond dinos)

Dr. Louis L. Jacobs, Southern Methodist University, Texas

Mr. Bobby King, Coon Creek Science Center, Tennessee

Dr. Ed Landing, New York State Paleontologist

Mr. Larry League, Dakota Dinosaur Museum, North Dakota

Dr. Spencer G. Lucas, New Mexico Museum of Natural History and Science

Dr. Bryn J. Mader, American Museum of Natural History, NYC

Mr. Russ McCarty, Florida Museum of Natural History

Dr. Greg McDonald, Hagerman Fossil Beds National Monument, Idaho

Mr. John David McFarland, Arkansas Geological Commission

Mr. Carlton S. Nash, Nash Dinosaur Museum, Massachusetts

Dr. John H. Ostrom, Peabody Museum of Natural History, Connecticut

Dr. David C. Parris, New Jersey State Museum of Natural History

Dr. J. Michael Parrish, University of Illinois

Mr. Andrew D. Redline, Carnegie Museum of Natural History, Pennsylvania

Mr. Paul Remeika, Anza Borrego Desert State Park, California

Dr. Albert E. Sanders, Charleston Museum, South Carolina

Mr. Vincent Santucci, Petrified Forest National Park (for sincere encouragement)

Dr. Judith Schiebout, Louisiana State University Museum of Geology

Dr. Kenneth L. Stadtman, Earth Science Museum, BYU, Utah

Dr. Klaus Westphal, University of Wisconsin Geology Museum

CONTENTS

PART TWO

YOUR DINO-SHOPPING GUIDE:
WHERE TO FIND GREAT DINOSAUR STUFF!   151

PART THREE

A DINO-IDENTIFIER: WHO'S WHO AMONG
DINOSAURS AND PREHISTORIC MAMMALS   173

AUTHOR'S NOTE

Writing this book was a labor of love. As the mother of two very energetic young dinosaur and fossil fans, there is one question I can count on hearing at every travel stop: "Are there any dinosaurs here?" I began to research this book so I could always answer that question.

My girls come by their dinosaur passion honestly. I first discovered dinosaurs when I was seven and a group of "life-size" dinosaur models came to Houston, Texas. They have been in my blood ever since.

After more than four years of research, I am confident the collection of U.S. and Canadian fossil stops you'll find here is nearly complete. I say "nearly" because I certainly may have missed a number of less obvious but incredible spots along the way. If your favorite site is overlooked, please write me in care of my publisher, John Wiley & Sons, Inc., and let me know.

Now you, too, will always know the answer to the question, "Are there any dinosaurs here?" Enjoy your prehistoric trekking!

—Kelly Milner Halls

HOW TO USE THIS BOOK

The heart of this book covers places you can go to see fascinating dinosaur and fossil material. Most of the sites provided here are suitable for all age ranges, although some of the digs and trails are for teenagers and up only.

Turn to Part One to find listings of the sites. They are listed alphabetically by state, followed by sites in Canada and then by traveling exhibits. For each, you'll find the name, address, and phone number, a brief description of what fossil treasures you'll find there, a rating, and information on the admission fee (if there is one), and facilities such as rest rooms, gift shops, food vendors, and wheelchair accessibility.

The rating icons mean the following:

 No regular paleo exhibit, but traveling exhibits are booked from time to time.

 Strictly for fossil fanatics. May not have much on display, but if you are nearby, consider the stop.

Worth the detour if you're a real fossil fan. Good paleo material, plus!

Worth the trip just for this. Fossil fans shouldn't miss it. Premium paleo goods you won't soon forget!

For admissions fees, I have given a range, since these change so frequently. The ranges are as follows:

Donation requested	No fee required, but donations help keep these sites alive. Give what you can.
Free	Exactly what it says —no charge!
Low	Fee is about $5 or less.
Medium	Fee is between $5 and $10.
High	Fee is over $10.

There are five general categories of sites you can enjoy. Each entry features an icon that lets you know which of the five kinds you are reading about. The icons are shown below, with their corresponding categories:

 Museums, science centers, and other indoor locations with exhibits

 State and national parks, national monuments, and other outdoor locations, most with a visitor's center and a staff

 Track sites, trails, and other outdoor sites that are less formal than state parks, and are often unstaffed

 Parks, roadside attractions, and other outdoor locations, often more Americana than true science

 Amusement parks

Each of the above types can be appreciated in different ways. Here are some tips on how to get the most out of each kind.

 Museums and Science Centers: Before taking a young child to one of these sites, you may want to discuss what you will see, and what kind of behavior is expected at a museum. It may be a good idea to write ahead for a brochure so you and your child can plan the visit together, and he or she can see that there are different levels, varied exhibits, and that there are such practical facilities as bathrooms and water fountains.

You may also consider thinking of questions to ask the child during your visit, to make the experience more enriching. How can we tell which dinosaurs were meat-eaters and which were plant-eaters? What is the difference between a regular plant and a fossilized one? Why do you think this dinosaur had such a long tail? Chances are, though, that your child will be the one with plenty of questions for you. Instead of answering as many as you know, why not try to help your child figure out the answers? You might try reading the available information about the exhibits or asking a nearby staff member to help you find answers to questions.

State and National Parks: State and national parks and national monuments are perfect for family visits. Many have things to see and do both indoors and outdoors, allowing kids to run around without hurting anything while still letting them appreciate indoor exhibits. You'll find park rangers and sometimes paleontologists who are usually more than happy to answer questions about their sites.

Track Sites and Trails: These outdoor sites tend to be less structured than museums or state parks. Here you'll often find just a marked trail—or sometimes an unmarked one—that will lead you to ancient dinosaur tracks that have been preserved over thousands of years, or perhaps to the site of a dig where fossils have been found. You will rarely find any staff to answer questions or guide you along your way. This kind of site is better for older children, as in many cases hiking and climbing are required. Often you'll need to call in advance of your visit to a town chamber of commerce to get directions to the site. They may give out maps—always ask. The reason many of these sites require a phone call is that the towns want to maintain some control over the flow of visitors and keep track of how many are visiting their treasures.

Make sure your family understands that "no staff" does not mean they can take things from the site, or leave a mess. It's important that we all work to preserve ancient sites so that we and others can enjoy them for years to come.

Parks and Roadside Attractions: At these sites you'll often find more fun than science, but what fun! At many of them you'll find that your children (or the adventurous adult!) can climb on the dinosaur models, pose for pictures, and generally play in a way that is unacceptable around precious "real" dinosaur fossils. You might not want to make a trip just for a site like this, but if your plans take you anywhere near one of these, your family is bound to enjoy the experience. And these sites are usually good photo opportunities, too.

To make the event more educational, you could have family members figure out ways that the fake dinosaurs are different from what scientists now know about real ones. But in general, it's probably best not to take these "fun only" sites too seriously.

Amusement Parks: While amusement park dinosaurs are often the least scientifically accurate of all, I just couldn't leave them out of this book. If you're a dino fan, you'll love to see your favorite creatures incorporated into rides and other attractions. Again, these dinos are not meant to be taken seriously at all.

If you want to own some dinosaur stuff of your own, please don't take anything you see at any of the sites listed. Instead, look in Part Two, the Dino-Shopping Guide, where you'll find sources for purchasing all kinds of dinosaur-related goodies, from party goods to real fossils.

If you're curious about just what the prehistoric creatures mentioned in the book might have looked like (prior to fossilization), don't miss Part Three, the Dino-Identifier. Rick Spears's masterful restoration illustrations will give you an accurate idea of just what you might have seen millions of years ago.

PART ONE

THE DINO-TREKKING SITES

ALABAMA

ANNISTON MUSEUM OF NATURAL HISTORY

 From dust to dinosaurs to early man, explore geologic history at this city-funded museum. Don't miss the unique diorama on prehistoric birds, a special attraction that illustrates the evolutionary tie of dinosaurs to birds.

800 Museum Drive
Anniston, AL 36202
(205) 237-6766

Admission: Low fee

Facilities: Rest rooms, gift shop

DISCOVERY 2000
RED MOUNTAIN MUSEUM

A mosasaur was a large lizard confined to the oceans. A skeletal version of this ancient sea serpent—all 15 feet of it—hangs from the Discovery 2000 ceiling of this museum. There's also the skull of an allosaur, a collection of *Dryptosaurus* bones, and a mystery meat-eater as yet unidentified, making this one of the best dinosaur collections in the South. But it's the Red Mountain Road Cut that makes this museum unique. A ⅓-mile slice of Alabama mountainside reveals the many layers of rock set down throughout geologic history. (See Curator's Corner.)

1421 22nd Street
 South
Birmingham, AL 35205
(205) 933-4142

Admission: Low fee

Facilities: Rest rooms, gift shop, food available

Allosaurus

CURATOR'S CORNER

SHERYL JONES

Public Relations/Marketing
Discovery 2000, Birmingham

"The Red Mountain Road Cut is a National Natural Landmark 210 feet deep, 410 feet wide at the top, and ⅓ mile long. We also have the most complete skeleton of a meat-eating dinosaur found east of the Mississippi (as of 1994). We call it the Montgomery Theropod. Research is still being done to identify exactly what kind of dinosaur it is. It may be in the tyrannosaur family like *Tyrannosaurus rex!*"

Author's Note: Today, it seems the land stays the same, day after day. But that's not true. Every minute, even every second, nature is changing the Earth. A pile of dust blows in the wind, from your driveway to the street. A hefty California earthquake reduces a freeway to gravel—in a few minutes' time. A sand castle is swept back into the sea. Those are all visible signs of natural change. When you consider how many millions of years have passed since life on earth began, you can begin to see how much things must have changed. Alabama's Red Mountain Road Cut is like a geological diary of those changes.

ALASKA

UNIVERSITY OF ALASKA MUSEUM

Scientists have only recently discovered how rich Alaska's prehistoric legacy might be. The University of Alaska Museum offers a good cross-section of native Alaskan fossils from dinosaurs (like *Pachyrhinosaurus* and *Edmontosaurus*) and prehistoric mammals including "Blue Babe," an ancient bison, and "Effie," a baby mammoth found frozen with muscle and skin still intact.

907 Yukon Drive
Fairbanks, AK
 99775-1200
(907) 474-7505

Admission: Donation requested

Facilities: Rest rooms, gift shop, food available

CURATOR'S CORNER

DR. ROLAND GANGLOFF

Paleontologist
University of Alaska Museum

"The University of Alaska Museum's paleontological collection currently numbers more than 30,000 specimens, including invertebrates—everything from sponges to ammonoids—and vertebrates. These fossils range in age from 700 million to a little less than 5,000 years old. Most of the vertebrate specimens are Late Cretaceous dinosaurs from the North Slope of Alaska, and Pleistocene mammals from various Alaskan locales.

"The dinosaur collection here got its start in 1985, from sites discovered in 1961. We have close to 5,000 skeletal elements, including tail vertebrae, upper arm bones, lower jaws, feet and leg bones. We've identified a total of seven different dinosaurs so far. The duckbill, *Edmontosaurus*, is the most commonly found Alaskan dinosaur.

"Paleontologists have found evidence of dinosaurs near Anchorage and near Black Lake on the Alaskan Peninsula, and recent exploration leads us to believe that there will be new finds on the North Slope. Dinosaur watchers should keep their eyes on Alaska for many new discoveries."

DOROTHY G. PAGE MUSEUM

This museum features an exhibit centered around a nodosaur skull recovered in the early 1990s by John Luster Sr. and his sons in the Alaskan wilderness. Though other museums across the country have copies of the skull, Mr. Luster insisted that the original be housed in Wasilla.

323 Main Street
Wasilla, AK 99687
(907) 373-9071

Admission: Low fee

Facilities: Rest rooms, gift shop

UNIVERSITY OF ALASKA/ANCHORAGE

This newly created public museum will feature a cast of a nodosaur and a full explanation of how the skull was retrieved and identified by a local resident. Also explored will be the great dinosaur potential of Alaska's North Slope, as well as Ice Age mammals, which are already a rich part of Alaska's known ancient history.

Anchorage, AK
(907) 786-1344

Admission: Donation requested

Facilities: Rest rooms, gift shop

Nodosaurus

ARIZONA

MUSEUM OF NORTHERN ARIZONA

The "spitter" in Hollywood's *Jurassic Park*—also known as *Dilophosaurus*—is the featured animal in this museum's "Walk Thru Time," a new exhibit with a rare 3-D skeleton/reproduction. The "real" half of this *Dilophosaurus*—the right side—was found less than fifty miles from the museum. The left side was made "almost real" by museum preparator Allen Tedrow. (See Curator's Corner.)

Fort Valley Road
P.O. Box 720
Flagstaff, AZ 86001
(602) 774-5211

Admission: Low fee

Facilities: Rest rooms, gift shop

PETRIFIED FOREST NATIONAL PARK

Huge petrified logs cover the landscape created by an ancient log jam along a prehistoric river at this national park. The visitors' center features the skeletons of a number of early dinosaurs, older even than *T. rex*. Among them are the Triassic phytosaurs, which were much like modern crocodiles. They thrived in ancient Arizona, then a tropical swamp. Fossil resources at Petrified Forest are so outstanding that a park paleontologist is on staff to keep them safe. Don't miss the park's Junior Ranger certification program.

6618 Petrified Forest Road
Holbrook, AZ 84028
(602) 524-6822

Admission: Low fee

Facilities: Rest rooms, gift shop, food available

MESA SOUTHWEST MUSEUM

This museum's recently formed Southwest Paleontology Club was designed for amateur fossil hunters and experts alike. The museum's "Dinosaurs in Arizona" display was joined in September 1993 by "Jurassic Arizona" (See Curator's Corner).

53 North MacDonald Street
Mesa, AZ 85201-7325
(602) 644-2230
(602) 644-2169

Admission: Low fee

Facilities: Rest rooms, gift shop

GRAND CANYON CAVERNS T. REX

The *Tyrannosaurus rex* model shown at this roadside attraction near the Grand Canyon Caverns is nearly twenty feet tall and more fun than fact. Made of sheet metal and concrete and painted "Bronto" green, it was built at a time when scientists felt dinosaurs could have roamed the Grand Canyon (123 miles away). Canyon bones turned out to be remains of more modern animals, but the popular statue did not become "extinct."

P.O. Box 180
Peach Springs, AZ
 86434
(602) 422-3223

Admission: Low fee

Facilities: Rest rooms, gift shop, food available

ARIZONA MUSEUM OF SCIENCE AND TECHNOLOGY

Dinosaurs are not the only subject covered at this museum, but dinosaur fossils are on exhibit here. Casts of both *Tyrannosaurus rex* and *Triceratops* skulls are on display, along with information on eight other dinosaur species.

80 North Street
Phoenix, AZ 85004
(602) 256-9388

Admission: Low fee

Facilities: Rest rooms, gift shop

MINERALOGICAL MUSEUM

Primarily devoted to the study of rocks and minerals—geology—this museum has a good collection of fossils native to Arizona along with information on how they relate to geological history.

University of Arizona
Tucson, AZ 85721
(602) 621-4227

Admission: Free

Facilities: Rest rooms, gift shop

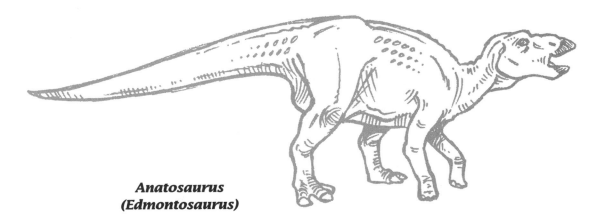

Anatosaurus
(Edmontosaurus)

CURATOR'S CORNER

ALLEN TEDROW

Paleontological Preparator
Museum of Northern Arizona

"Having never visited a natural-history museum as a child, I received my first dinosaur thrills from movies like *King Kong, When Dinosaurs Ruled the Earth,* and *One Million Years B.C.,*" Mr. Tedrow remembers. "I always had a strong interest in the natural sciences, and as I recall, public television was key in 'fueling the fire.'

"At twenty-five, I entered college and took courses in natural history and geology, and later in historical geology, which led me in the direction of paleontology. I was fascinated by the tremendous diversity of life through time, and studied all these forms with equal zeal.

Somewhat later, my focus shifted to the study of vertebrate fossils, and mammals in particular. Yet I find myself working with and learning more about dinosaurs and less about fossil mammals as the years go by.

"Clearly, dinosaurs have an irresistible and universal appeal—captivating children, adults, and scientists alike. We in the museum field know that we must provide stimulating and informative exhibits for the general public. In turn, we realize many rewards, as funding for continued research comes either directly or indirectly from an enthusiastic public."

ARKANSAS

DINOSAUR WORLD

 Roam this family camping/RV park with one-hundred life-size Americana (fun, not real) models including thirty-four dinosaurs, which give fishing and camping a prehistoric feel. Enjoy a day trip or hook up your RV for a longer stay. There's also a miniature golf course.

Route 2, P.O. Box 408
Eureka Springs, AR
 72632
(501) 253-8113

Admission: Various fees

Facilities: Rest rooms, gift shop, food available

UNIVERSITY MUSEUM

 "Mystery-asaurus," an early crocodile, is one of several Arkansas fossil displays at this small, university history museum. Other historic artifacts are featured in addition to the geological treasures.

University of Arkansas,
 Room 202
Garland Street
Fayetteville, AR 72701
(501) 575-3555

Admission: Donation requested

Facilities: Rest rooms, gift shop, food available

MID-AMERICA MUSEUM

No regular fossil exhibits are featured at this hands-on, high-energy museum, but traveling dinosaur exhibits are often booked. Call ahead if you plan a trip to Arkansas, to check the museum's dinosaur schedule.

400 Mid-America
 Boulevard
Mid-America Park
Hot Springs National
 Park, AR 71913
(501) 767-3461

Admission: Moderate fee

Facilities: Rest rooms, gift shop, food available

ARKANSAS GEOLOGICAL COMMISSION

 Although this is a state office designed to serve and inform residents and visitors about Arkansas geology, they have put together a good collection of paleontological exhibits that they welcome visitors to explore. Included is a model of *Ornithomimus*, tracks, and much more.

3815 West Roosevelt
 Road
Little Rock, AR 72204
(501) 663-9714

Admission: Free

Facilities: Rest rooms

ARKANSAS GEOLOGICAL LEARNING CENTER

This learning center provides classes on the geological/fossil history of the region, and on fossil preparation. School groups from Arkansas are the most common visitors, but any interested individual or group can join in the fossil fun with just a telephone call to the Arkansas Geological Commission. A warehouse of fossil treasure already collected is on display.

3815 West Roosevelt Road
Little Rock, AR 72204
(501) 663-9714

Admission: Free

Facilities: Rest rooms, gift shop

ARKANSAS MUSEUM OF SCIENCE AND HISTORY

A life-size statue of a local ostrich-like dinosaur, *Ornithomimus*—discovered by Arkansas farmer Joe Friday—is on display in the lobby of this museum of family fun. The "Tower of Time" exhibit helps illustrate historic time periods. Also on display are dinosaur track castings and an exhibit explaining how fossils are formed. Dinosaur birthday parties and marionettes make this museum especially fun. Don't miss the gift shop, specially stocked with inexpensive dinosaur souvenirs.

MacArthur Park
Little Rock, AR 72202
(501) 324-9231

Admission: Various fees

Facilities: Rest rooms, gift shop, food available

CITY PARK DINOSAURS

Concrete dinosaur statues dot the Mountainburg city park next to City Hall. Created nearly thirty years ago by a local artist/resident, they are great climbing fun, even if they aren't accurate by modern scientific standards. There is parking available, and terrific photo opportunities!

U.S. Highway 71
Mountainburg City Hall
P.O. Box 433
Mountainburg, AR 72946
(501) 369-2791

Admission: Free

Facilities: None

COUNTY SEAT/COURTHOUSE TRACKS

When the Briar Gypsum plant uncovered dinosaur tracks, they halted mining long enough for well-known paleontologists, including Utah's state paleontologist, Dr. David Gillette, to study them and make copies of what has been called more of a "trample way" than a trackway. One copy is on display outside the Nashville county courthouse. You can park at the courthouse and examine the tracks.

421 North Main
Nashville, AR 71852
(501) 845-7500
(directions only)

Admission: Free

Facilities: Rest rooms

ARKANSAS OIL AND BRINE MUSEUM

 This small museum is planning a new fossil exhibit, but has no such display at the time of this writing. If you plan a trip nearby, call ahead to see if they've made any progress.

3853 Smackover Highway
Smackover, AR 71762
(501) 725-2877

Admission: Low fee

Facilities: Rest rooms, gift shop

CURATOR'S CORNER

JOHN DAVID MCFARLAND

Arkansas Geological Commission

Mr. McFarland gives three reasons why fossils are important: "First and foremost is their endless intrinsic fascination. Many of them are quite beautiful in form and in design. But beyond that, to touch and contemplate the remains of some creature that lived and breathed millions of years ago is to come face to face with your own place in the cosmos.

"Second, fossils tell time. Our observations over the years have established a clear and relatively precise chronology [time sequence] of fossil species. Some plant and animal groups evolved very rapidly. Specific species within these groups existed for relatively short spans of geologic time, and therefore are only found in rocks of a particular age. Geologists can use these 'marker' fossils to tell the age of rocks they are found in.

"Finally, fossils give clues to the environment in which they lived. Just as modern creatures are sensitive to various environmental influences, so were the plants and animals of the past. If we learn something about the way an organism lived, and the limits of its tolerance to various environmental factors, then we may be able to understand many of the details of that long-ago time.

"Although dinosaurs tend to grab the public's attention, they are not necessarily the most important of fossils. It is the invertebrates that most often supply the important data that geologists need to understand the age and environment of those ancient rocks. For example, it is invertebrate microfossils that oil and gas geologists use in their never-ending quest for new petroleum discoveries. Only microscopic organisms are small enough to be found within the rock chips brought up by an oil drill—large shells, bones, and so on are ground away.

"By studying these microfossils, geologists can often tell if they are drilling in the right place or at the right depth. Without microfossils, gasoline would be far more expensive."

CALIFORNIA

DISNEYLAND

Fantasia-like dinosaurs are part of a train ride through history at Disneyland. It's a "sit down and rest your feet" ride. But don't expect the models to reflect modern scientific theory. These are the product of the technology and thinking of the 1950s. Today—fantasy, not science.

13135 Harbor
  Boulevard
Anaheim, CA 92803
(714) 999-4000

Admission: High fee

Facilities: Rest rooms, gift shop, food available

MUSEUM OF NATURAL HISTORY

The University of California at Berkeley is world-famous for discoveries such as Dr. George O. Ponier's finding DNA from ancient insects in amber (said to be one of many inspirational forces behind Michael Crichton's *Jurassic Park*). But the museum has much to its credit apart from dinosaur fiction. Don't miss this museum live—you may have seen it featured many times on public television.

University of California
Berkeley, CA 94720
(510) 642-1821

Admission: Low fee

Facilities: Rest rooms, gift shop, food available

ANZA BORREGO DESERT STATE PARK

This park boasts fossil remains that range from the Mid- to Early Pliocene ages, 4½ million years ago to the Pleistocene age, just ½ million years ago. The fossils are both early terrestrial ones (those confined to the earth, as opposed to flying or living in water) and seagoing vertebrates (animals with backbones) and invertebrates such as clams and snails. Mammals from four different time periods have been discovered here as well—a rare occurrence in the field of paleontology.

P.O. Box 299
Borrego Springs, CA
  92004
(619) 767-5311

Admission: Low fee

Facilities: Rest rooms, gift shop

KNOTT'S BERRY FARM

This amusement park features a time machine out of control that takes a wrong turn and sends riders back in time 200 million years, to prehistoric jungles. Lifelike, moving dinosaurs make this a worthy fantasy adventure. This is also a full-sized amusement park complete with a backward-loop coaster.

8039 Beach Boulevard
Buena Park, CA 90620
(714) 827-1776

Admission: Moderate fee

Facilities: Rest rooms, gift shop, food available

DINOSAUR DELIGHT

If you've seen Pee-wee Herman's first movie, *Pee-wee's Big Adventure*, you've seen this roadside dinosaur. It isn't science, it's "Dinny"—a 150-foot-long *Brontosaurus* (the animal's former name; it is now called *Apatosaurus*) created in 1964. You can visit the museum and gift shop in his belly. It took more than ten years to convert 1,200 bags of concrete and an old bridge into this dinosaur. The nearby *Tyrannosaurus rex* is about sixty-five feet tall.

P.O. Box 23
 (on Route I-10)
Cabazon, CA 92230
(909) 849-8309

Admission: Free

Facilities: Rest rooms, gift shop, food available

PETRIFIED FOREST

California's Petrified Forest interpretive center has a great deal of information on ancient life on display, as well as two dinosaur fossils and, as the name indicates, petrified plant life.

4100 Petrified Forest
 Road
Calistoga, CA 94515
(707) 942-6667

Admission: Low fee

Facilities: Rest rooms, gift shop

CHAPMAN'S GEM AND MINERAL MUSEUM

Three thousand square feet of gems, minerals, petrified palms, and fossilized plant and animal life are on display at this museum. A huge gift shop has many fossil specimens to look at or buy.

P.O. Box 852 (south of
 Fortuna on Route 101)
Fortuna, CA 95540
(707) 725-4732

Admission: Free

Facilities: Rest rooms, gift shop, food available

NATURAL HISTORY MUSEUM OF LOS ANGELES

 Camptosaurus, *Allosaurus*, and *Tyrannosaurus rex* make up a part of this museum's world-class collection of reconstructed dinosaur skeletons, but prehistoric mammals are also represented in great number, thanks to the nearby La Brea Tar Pits.

900 Exposition Boulevard
Los Angeles, CA 90007
(213) 744-3426

Admission: Low fee

Facilities: Rest rooms, gift shop, food available

GEORGE C. PAGE MUSEUM LA BREA DISCOVERIES

 Once you have seen the legendary La Brea Tar Pits outside the museum, you will never look at hot blacktopped streets the same way again. Called the "Death Trap of the Ages," the sticky tar was where thousands of Ice Age mammals and birds met their deaths. More than one hundred tons (200,000 pounds) of fossilized bones have been recovered so far, and many of these are on display at the museum. There are also interpretive exhibits, explaining how the animals might have been trapped, how their bones were preserved, and how paleontologists prepared the bones for study and display.

5801 Wilshire Boulevard
Los Angeles, CA 90036
(213) 936-2230

Admission: Low fee

Facilities: Rest rooms, gift shop, food available

LUBKING GEM AND MINERAL COLLECTION THE PORTERVILLE LIBRARY

More than 5,500 different minerals, gems, and fossils are on display in this extensive rock collection, but don't expect more than tiny bits and pieces. The Porterville Library houses this huge collection, but within two years it will be moved to the Porterville Community College, so call ahead to be sure you visit the correct location.

41 West Thurman Avenue
Porterville, CA 93257
(209) 784-0177

Admission: Low fee

Facilities: Rest rooms, gift shop

SAN BERNADINO COUNTY MUSEUM

Fossils are part of the Earth Science exhibit at this museum. But don't miss the exhibits on archaeology and anthropology to learn more about prehistoric humans. Regular field trips are scheduled to nearby trackways, thanks to the Earth Science Curator's special interests and skills.

2024 Orange Tree Lane
Redlands, CA 92374
(909) 798-8570

Admission: Moderate fee

Facilities: Rest rooms, gift shop

JURUPA MOUNTAIN CULTURAL CENTER

Seven dinosaur models dot the hillside above Jurupa Mountain Cultural Center. Every Saturday morning, field trips called "Collecting Rocks with Dinosaurs," are conducted for children. Museum staff members hike with the groups to identify the dinosaurs (built by children more than ten years ago), and collect and identify rocks and minerals. Kids and adults can participate in "The Fossil Shack," a program also offered on Saturdays, in which participants are given a fossil common to the area to study, prepare, identify and keep.

7621 Granite Hill Drive
Riverside, CA 92509
(714) 685-5818

Admission: Moderate fee

Facilities: Rest rooms, gift shop

SAN DIEGO MUSEUM OF NATURAL HISTORY

Nodosaurus is the only true dinosaur fossil ever found in San Diego, and a cast (copy) is on display at this museum, along with a replica of an *Allosaurus* skeleton.

1788 El Prado
Balboa Park
P.O. Box 1390
San Diego, CA 92112
(619) 232-3821

Admission: Low fee

Facilities: Rest rooms, gift shop

SANTA BARBARA MUSEUM OF NATURAL HISTORY

 An entire exhibit is devoted to fossils at this small museum, including marine invertebrates (animals without backbones) and a mammoth and other mammals. The grounds are famous for elaborate, lush landscaping.

2559 Puesta de Sol Road
Santa Barbara, CA 92112
(805) 682-3821

Admission: Low fee

Facilities: Rest rooms, gift shop

CALIFORNIA ACADEMY OF SCIENCES

 The Natural History Museum is only a small part of what this amazing educational center has to offer. See the Steinhard Aquarium and the Morrison Planetarium while you're there. Dinosaurs represented include *Deinonychus*, a deadly meat-eater.

Golden Gate Park
San Francisco, CA 94118
(415) 750-7145

Admission: Moderate fee

Facilities: Rest rooms, gift shop, food available

SKULLDUGGERY

Very few retail establishments are included in this section of the book. But Skullduggery is known for creating world-class fossil replicas—everything from dinosaurs to early man. Prices range from an eleven-inch *Tyrannosaurus rex* tooth, which sells for under fifty dollars, to very expensive full skeletal casts. The Skullduggery showroom is open to the public.

624 South B Street
Tustin, CA 92680
1(800) 3-FOSSIL
(1-800-336-7745)

Admission: Free (but items are for sale)

Facilities: Rest rooms

Deinonychus

CURATOR'S CORNER

PAUL REMEIKA
Park Paleontologist-Ranger
Anza Borrego Desert State Park

GEORGE JEFFERSON
Staff Paleontologist
Anza Borrego Desert State Park

Imagine a 600,000-acre field to study, a natural classroom with millions of fossils to find and understand from the paleontological history of nearly five million years. Imagine it was your job to uncover the secrets just beneath the surface of the Earth and share that discovery with people the world over. Imagine you had studied for more than ten years to prepare for the work, and now, after all that hard work, you get paid for what you love most—digging fossils.

If you can envision all this, you have some idea what it is like to wake up in Paul Remeika's and George Jefferson's shoes—most days, anyway. Working at Anza Borrego Desert State Park is, for these staff paleontologists, like a dream come true. As George Jefferson describes it, Anza Borrego is a sort of grab-bag of

paleo knowledge. Geologically speaking, it is "a stratigraphic illustration of a rift valley, much like those found in East Africa." Translation? The land has been pushed up and shifted by continental drift—slow movement of the Earth's landmasses. As the planet's surface folds and buckles under stress, ancient rocks and fossils are exposed. At Anza Borrego, the exposed fossils span 4½ million years and four different, distinct mammalian ages. That's rare.

The chance to study these ages side by side is quite a treat for paleontologists and amateur fossil-hunters alike. On a single hillside you might find a bed of marine clam fossils along with evidence of mammals. Hike to another, and find a marine vertebrate such as an ancient whale.

COLORADO

UNIVERSITY SCIENCE MUSEUM

The famous dinosaur expert Dr. Robert T. Bakker was once on staff at this museum. Though his rugged face is seldom seen in its halls today, his influence is ever present in the paleo collection, which includes an excellent *Triceratops* skull and many other specimens. But don't miss the museum of entomology (the study of insects) also at this location.

University of Colorado
  at Boulder
Campus Box 218
Boulder, CO 80309
(303) 492-6892

Admission: Donation requested

Facilities: Rest rooms, gift shop, food nearby, wheelchair accessible

GARDEN PARK PALEONTOLOGICAL SOCIETY DIG SITE AND DISPLAY

In 1993, the oldest known dinosaur egg was found at the Garden Park dig site in Canon City. But amazing discoveries aren't new to the region. Since the time of the rival nineteenth-century paleontologists Edward Drinker Cope and Othniel Marsh, Canon City has yielded fossils worthy of notice and display in museums across the country. But now, thanks to the Garden Park Paleontological Society, what was once an ancient firehouse now houses hot fossils! And if finances allow, The Dinosaur Discovery Center will soon open to expand Canon City's fossil offerings to a display worthy of the town's place in paleontological history. Call the society for a progress report and for directions to both the dig site and the display.

P.O. Box 313
Canon City, CO
  81215-0313
(719) 275-9205 (ask for Linda Carlson, Public Relations)

Admission: Donation requested

Facilities: Rest rooms, gift shop, wheelchair accessible

Stegosaurus

DINOSAUR DIG

Two of the largest dinosaur bones ever recovered came from this active dinosaur quarry. Visitors are welcome to watch professional and volunteer paleontologists work to collect, among other things, *Supersaurus* and *Ultrasaurus* fossils from the rocky terrain. Both species are said to have weighed more than eighty tons and to have stood over fifty feet tall.

Delta County Tourism
224 Main Street
Delta, CO 81416
(800) 228-7009, or
 (303) 874-8616

Admission: Free (tour guides are available for a fee, upon advance request)

Facilities: None

DENVER MUSEUM OF NATURAL HISTORY

Though this Denver museum has always had a lot to offer in the fossil realm, the scheduled 1995 opening of its $6.6-million "Prehistoric Journey" exhibit should boost the paleo treasury to outstanding new heights. More than five dinosaur skeletons, including *Diplodocus*, *Stegosaurus* (the Colorado state fossil), *Coelophysis*, *Lambeosaurus*, and a *Tyrannosaurus rex* mount designed by Robert Bakker (and made all the more striking by a replica of John Gurche's remarkable mural behind the bones), are just the beginning. A fossil prep lab, dinosaur models set in lifelike dioramas, and displays on ancient mammals and prehistoric man will all be included in the exciting exhibit.

2001 Colorado
 Boulevard
Denver, CO 80205
(303) 370-6357

Admission: Low fee

Facilities: Rest rooms, gift shop, food available, wheelchair accessible

DICK'S ROCK MUSEUM

This rock shop and museum is a favorite stop among locals, en route to Estes Park. A great selection of rocks, minerals, crystals, and fossils is for sale in one half of the rustic building. The other half houses a museum complete with trilobites, coprolites (dinosaur poop), and hundreds of other wonderful specimens. Always mindful of the limited purchasing power of kids, Dick's features many treasures selling for under five dollars.

490 Moraine Route
Estes Park, CO 80517
(303) 586-4180

Admission: Free (but items are for sale at a wide range of prices)

Facilities: Rest rooms, gift shop

WATER WORLD/JOURNEY TO THE CENTER OF THE EARTH

Already a great water park, this Colorado wet spot recently added a $2.2-million dinosaur adventure to their list of "rides." Four-person float tubes swirl through a giant "crack" in the Earth's surface on their way to a secret cache of ancient life. Featured, by way of robotic animation models, are *Triceratops*, *Tyrannosaurus rex*, the pterosaur *Quetzalcoatlus*, plesiosaurs, and sea turtles. The ride may be scary for kids under ten years of age, but don't miss it if both water slides and dinosaurs are your personal favorites.

1850 West 89th Avenue
Federal Heights, CO
  80221
(303) 427-7873, or
  (303) 650-7521

Admission: Moderate fee

Facilities: Rest rooms, gift shop, partially wheelchair accessible

FLORISSANT FOSSIL BEDS NATIONAL MONUMENT

Not dinosaurs, but prehistoric bugs and petrified tree stumps as wide as mobile homes litter the land around the well-staffed visitor center at this national monument. Inside are several good educational exhibits and hundreds of carefully preserved insect fossil specimens. Several easy hiking trails, marked with interpretive signs, help you take a journey through ancient time, without a time machine. Even without dinosaurs, this is worth the side trip.

P.O. Box 185
Florissant, CO 80816
(719) 748-3253

Admission: Low fee

Facilities: Rest rooms, gift shop, wheelchair accessible

DEVIL'S CANYON SCIENCE AND LEARNING CENTER DINAMATION INTERNATIONAL SOCIETY

Only recently added to the region's wealth of dinosaur attractions, this cooperative effort between Dinamation— a company well known for the creation of animated dinosaur models—and the city of Fruita is not to be missed! There are a number of robotic dinosaurs (including *Apatosaurus*, *Stegosaurus*, *Allosaurus*, *Dilophosaurus*, and *Utahraptor*), as well as exhibits on geological subjects including glaciers, volcanoes, and earthquakes. A working fossil lab adds a solid educational appeal to the dinosaurian fun. Ice Age mammals and prehistoric sea creatures are also a part of the learning center's experience.

550 Crossroads Court
Fruita, CO 81521
(303) 858-7282

Admission: Moderate fee

Facilities: Rest rooms, gift shop, food nearby, wheelchair accessible

CURATOR'S CORNER

BRENDA BECHTER

Curator of Education
Museum of Western Colorado

Elmer Riggs discovered an *Apatosaurus* skeleton in 1901—the same skeleton long displayed at the Field Museum of Natural History in Chicago. But the tail was missing upon excavation. Bones from other digs filled in the missing pieces for years. But in 1991–1992, the Museum of Western Colorado set out to solve the mystery of the missing tail.

A team of dedicated professional and amateur paleontologists searched Riggs Hill for the bones. After months of tedious work, only five tailbones were recovered, but the mystery was solved. Fossil evidence showed that a prehistoric stream had washed away the missing *Apatosaurus* tailbones sometime between the time it died and the time scientists came across the skeleton, millions of years later.

MUSEUM OF WESTERN COLORADO/ DINOSAUR VALLEY

Somewhat dwarfed by the new Devil's Canyon Science and Learning Center, this museum is still worthy of the highest rating. Five lifelike animated scale models, as well as "death pose" dinosaur skeletons and a working fossil prep lab, help to make this Grand Junction's best dinosaur museum.

P.O. Box 20000-5020
Grand Junction, CO
81502-5020
(303) 242-9210

Admission: Low fee

Facilities: Rest rooms, gift shop, wheelchair accessible

RABBIT VALLEY RESEARCH NATURE AREA/TRAIL THRU TIME

If you're willing to hike just under two miles, you'll see a historic trail littered with more than a dozen *Camarasaurus* bones at this nature center. Plan on about an hour and a half to finish the hike, and don't underestimate Colorado weather. Summers are HOT in Grand Junction, and other seasons can be unpredictable. Be prepared!

P.O. Box 20000-5020
Grand Junction, CO
81502
(303) 242-0971

Admission: Free

Facilities: None

RIGGS HILL TRAIL / DINOSAUR HILL TRAIL

These separate trails are both overseen by the Museum of Western Colorado. The staff will provide you with a map. Like the Trail Thru Time, they are "on the scene" historical paleontological dig sites, left much the way they must have appeared to the scientists who excavated many key dinosaur finds here at the turn of the century. Thirty to forty-five minutes should be ample time to complete each three-quarter-mile trail. Elmer Riggs discovered the fossil-rich sites in 1900. Eight interpretive trailside markers explain the finds at Riggs Hill. Ten markers dot the trail at Dinosaur Hill.

Museum of Western Colorado
P.O. Box 20000-5020
Grand Junction, CO 81502
(303) 242-0971

Admission: Free

Facilities: Rest rooms

DINOSAUR TRAILS OF PURGATORY/PICKET WIRE CANYONLANDS

This site is considered one of the most amazing dinosaur trackways in the world. Approximately 1,300 tracks, laid down in four different layers of rock, make this the longest Jurassic trackway yet known in North America. The tracks were ignored for a time after their discovery in 1935, because they were considered too difficult to reach on foot, and you can now see them by guided tour only. Call the number listed above in advance of your visit for details. This is not a hike for beginners—you'll be facing more than sixteen miles of hard trail. But if you are physically and mentally prepared for the trip, you'll see a sight you won't soon forget.

P.O. Box 817
1321 East Third Street
La Juinta, CO 80150
(719) 384-2181

Admission: Hiking is free; there is a moderate charge for a guided tour in a four-wheel-drive vehicle.

Facilities: None

DINOSAUR RIDGE FIELD TRIP/FRIENDS OF DINOSAUR RIDGE

P.O. Box 564
Morrison, CO 80465
(303) 697-1873

Admission: Donation requested

Facilities: Rest rooms

 If Dinosaur Trails of Purgatory's strenuous trail sounds intimidating, consider instead a trip to Dinosaur Ridge in the Denver suburb of Morrison. In a space of about a mile—all accessible from your vehicle—you'll see very authentic and well-marked dinosaur tracks, fossilized rock bulges made by *Apatosaurus* groups sinking in seaside mud, and a great deal more evidence of prehistoric life. Founder Robert Raynolds recently opened a visitor center in a nearby farmhouse, and hopes to expand the Friends of Dinosaur Ridge's offerings to include educational fossil outreaches for urban school children.

MORRISON NATURAL HISTORY MUSEUM

P.O. Box 564
Morrison, CO 80465
(303) 697-1873

Admission: Donation requested

Facilities: Rest rooms, gift shop, partially wheelchair accessible

Run by an all-volunteer staff that once also administered Friends of Dinosaur Ridge (see above), the Morrison Natural History Museum is now independent in its effort to bring Morrison's rich natural history into perspective for visitors. Although dinosaur and other ancient fossils currently make up the lion's share of exhibits, the staff hopes to expand more modern natural resources as time and money permit. Don't be fooled by the rustic exterior. This museum has some impressive material to explore, including *Stegosaurus* fossils still encased in rock. Visitors, with the able assistance of trained volunteer fossil preparators, can try their hand at chipping stubborn rock from fragile dinosaur bone.

Apatosaurus

CURATOR'S CORNER

DR. LINDA CARLSON

Chairman/Public Relations
Garden Park Paleontological Society

"Over 800 pounds of rock covered in plaster was ready to go from a mountainside to a museum fossil lab, thanks to dedicated but dirty work put in by volunteers from the Garden Park Paleontological Society, the Bureau of Land Management, and the Denver Museum of Natural History, over a period of three hot weeks in July 1993. Carefully attached to a cable and hook, the 'bundle' was cheered by onlookers as it was lifted from the ground onto a huge truck for its journey to Denver. 'We're here to catch the eggs if the cable breaks,' volunteers sitting downhill joked.

"Yes, this slab was in fact one of the oldest known dinosaur nests ever found— filled with layer after layer of ancient eggs. 'I think I have three different layers of eggs,' said Karen Alf, the tiny paleontologist from the Denver Museum of Natural History. 'There are nine eggs I know of that have been partially exposed, and there will probably be more in the layers beneath.'

"These were the 145-million-year-old eggs of a *Dryosaurus*—a small plant-eater common to Colorado. But eggs were only part of the find. 'We found a juvenile dinosaur bone here,' the paleontologist said. Finding a juvenile bone so near the nest suggests that dinosaurs may have formed social 'families.' According to Alf, 'It is the first evidence that juveniles were still living in the nest area.'

CONNECTICUT

POWDER HILL DINOSAUR PARK

This is an unstaffed park with unique dinosaur tracks that you can explore on your own. Write or call the Middlefield Chamber of Commerce for directions and details. And please enjoy these and all unstaffed sites responsibly so they will be well preserved for generations to come.

c/o Chamber of
  Commerce
393 Main Street
Middlefield, CT 06455
(203) 347-6924

Admission: Free

Facilities: Rest rooms

PEABODY MUSEUM OF NATURAL HISTORY

If you've ever watched a dinosaur documentary, you've probably seen the Peabody Museum's world-famous mural and world-class paleontological collection. The first *Brontosaurus* (now known as *Apatosaurus*) skeleton ever mounted is still on display—all seventy feet of it. The Great Hall of Dinosaurs features *Stegosaurus*, *Camptosaurus*, *Anatosaurus*, *Triceratops*, *Tyrannosaurus rex*, *Centrosaurus*, *Chasmosaurus*, and *Torosaurus*, as well as a model of *Deinonychus*, a meat-eater discovered by the museum's recently retired curator of paleontology, Dr. John H. Ostrom (see Curator's Corner).

Yale University
170 Whitney Avenue
New Haven, CT 06511
(203) 432-3775

Admission: Low fee

Facilities: Rest rooms, gift shop, food available, wheelchair accessible

DINOSAUR STATE PARK

You can make a real plaster casting of an actual dinosaur track within the domed visitor center at this state park. But bring your own plaster of paris, liquid cooking oil, and materials for cleanup, if you want this amazing keepsake. The tracks are from the Jurassic period, making this the true Jurassic Park. Just which dinosaur left the tracks is uncertain, but *Dilophosaurus* is the popular favorite—the closest known match. A life-size model of *Dilophosaurus* is on display. The outside exhibits and the visitor center are freshly remodeled (as of the summer of 1993).

West Street
Rocky Hill, CT 06067
(203) 529-5816

Admission: Low fee

Facilities: Rest rooms, gift shop, wheelchair accessible

CONNECTICUT STATE MUSEUM OF HISTORY

Plesiosaur and ichthyosaur fossil casts and a few tracks are the only ancient offerings at this museum. But don't miss the "Interactive Videoplace," with twenty life-size video games. These giant games are literally world-famous, traveling to museums around the world when they're not "at home" in Storrs, Connecticut. See exhibits on Woodland Indians, hawks, and owls, and enjoy monthly festivals.

University of
  Connecticut
Route 195
Storrs, CT 06269-3023
(203) 486-4460

Admission: Low fee

Facilities: Rest rooms, gift shop, wheelchair accessible

CURATOR'S CORNER

DR. JOHN H. OSTROM

Retired Curator
Peabody Museum at Yale University

Dr. Ostrom discovered and named a new dinosaur species, *Deinonychus*—a small but deadly meat-eater—in the summer of 1964. This is his own account of that remarkable find.

"The day of the discovery, I left our field camp at Cashen Ranch on the Crow Indian Reservation in Montana, and set out in our field vehicle with my assistant, Grant Meyer. Our objective was to check out and assess a dozen new sites. By noontime I was disappointed, because none of them seemed very promising, and I had decided not to excavate any of them [the] next year.

"After driving for more than forty-five minutes, we reached a very colorful butte isolated from the main Cloverly outcrop, and started walking along its north slope. Grant was about one pace ahead of me, when I saw an unbelievable object about ten feet in front of him. A very distinctive claw—just lying on the slope. I bumped against Grant as I dashed by him, almost knocking him down the slope. He laughed at me, but by then he saw why I was in such a rush.

"We knelt side by side, just looking at that beautiful claw—almost perfectly preserved. Then we began to see bone fragments nearby, and then more fragments scattered down the slope. Then, just a couple of inches from the first claw, I saw a less obvious, much smaller claw, of a different shape. I had never seen anything like this before. Was it part of a skeleton? I told myself, 'Don't touch anything. Photograph the site first. Then scour the area to gather every fragment.' Only then did Grant and I hunker down and slowly, very delicately, begin probing the weathered surface in the hopes that more, unweathered bones remained. The rest, what followed from our discovery on the last of the 1964 field season—August 29, 1964—is history.

"There is the moment, just as I remember it. I knew at once that our find was brand-new—as it proved to be—and so very different."

DELAWARE

Delaware's fossils and dinosaurs—WHERE ARE YOU? We couldn't find any "official" fossil locales open to the public in Delaware. However, the Delaware Geological Survey might be able to help you find a local paleontological organization to contact for collection field trips. Write to:

>Dr. Tom Picket
>Delaware Geological Survey
>University of Delaware
>Newark, DE 19716
>(302) 831-2833

And don't miss contacting the Delaware Mineralogical Society. Several active fossil-collection groups have formed through this statewide organization. Write to:

>Delaware Mineralogical Society, Inc.
>P.O. Box 533
>Newark, DE 19715-30327

If you find a great dig site or fossil club in Delaware, write to me, and let me in on the good news!

Archaeopteryx

DISTRICT OF COLUMBIA

THE SMITHSONIAN INSTITUTION'S NATIONAL MUSEUM OF NATURAL HISTORY

Tenth Street and
  Constitution Avenue
Washington, DC 20560
(202) 357-1300

Admission: Low fee

Facilities: Rest rooms, gift shop, food available, wheelchair accessible

There is a reason this museum (along with every museum under the Smithsonian banner) is world-famous. Beginning with Uncle Beazley—a *Triceratops* model named after a best-selling children's book—the National Museum has a very impressive group of dinosaur exhibits. *Tyrannosaurus rex*, *Diplodocus*, *Stegosaurus*, and many, many more dinosaurs are displayed in one form or another, along with a working paleontological lab and wonderful exhibits on ancient marine and mammalian life-forms as well. If you love ancient creatures and plan a trip to Washington, D.C., it would be a crime to miss this museum.

CURATOR'S CORNER

DR. MICHAEL BRETT-SURMAN

Paleontologist
National Museum of Natural History

Before Dr. Michael Brett-Surman was on staff at the National Museum of Natural History, he was a kid like everyone else. And although he was awestruck by the *T. rex* he saw as a child at the American Museum of Natural History in New York City— "One look," he says, "and I was hypnotized"—it wasn't until college that he realized dinosaurs would be his life's work.

He knew he wanted to work in a museum, where "everything is right there at your fingertips." But as he studied the history of our planet, he found that "the farther back in time, the more interesting things got." The famed fossil hunter Barnham Brown, who helped guarantee the American Museum of Natural History paleontological glory by depositing his vast collection of fossil specimens there, is just one of Dr. Brett-Surman's heros. He has earned a reputation of his own, however, teaching Smithsonian-sponsored field courses, maintaining the National Museum's fossil resources and reputation as one of the world's foremost paleo storehouses. In fact, when it comes to heroes, they don't come much more qualified—or much nicer—than Dr. Michael Brett-Surman.

FLORIDA

BREVARD MUSEUM OF HISTORY AND NATURAL SCIENCE

Some fossils are on display at this museum. Keep in mind, however, that Florida was under water during the time of the dinosaurs. But even without dinosaurs, the "Kid Room" and park trails are great fun to explore.

2201 Michigan Avenue
Cocoa, FL 32926-5618
(407) 632-1830

Admission: Low fee

Facilities: Rest rooms, gift shop

MUSEUM OF ART AND SCIENCE

This museum features a special section on "prehistory" that includes fossils native to the area. The state was under an ancient sea when the dinosaurs lived, but prehistoric sea life was abundant, and is reflected in the fossil record and display here.

1040 Museum
  Boulevard
Daytona Beach, FL
  32114
(904) 255-0285

Admission: Low fee

Facilities: Rest rooms, gift shop

FLORIDA MUSEUM OF NATURAL HISTORY

Experts say this museum is one of the top ten paleontological museums in the United States. Its extensive collection focuses, however, on early mammals and marine animal fossils rather than on dinosaurs. Many specimens come from a famous fossil location known as the Love Bone Bed (see Curator's Corner).

Museum Road
Gainesville, FL 32611
(904) 392-1721

Admission: Low fee

Facilities: Rest rooms, gift shop, wheelchair accessible

MUSEUM OF SCIENCE AND HISTORY

A full *Allosaurus* skeleton is the top dinosaur feature at this museum. But a few fossils from other Florida locales are also exhibited.

1025 Museum Circle
Jacksonville, FL
  32207-9854
(904) 396-7062

Admission: Low fee

Facilities: Rest rooms, gift shop, wheelchair accessible

THE DINO-TREKKING SITES 29

CURATOR'S CORNER

RUSS MCCARTY

Senior Biological Scientist and Head of Preparation Lab
Florida Museum of Natural History/University of Florida

"Florida is an exotic place," says Mr. McCarty. "In the late Paleozoic Era, the major continents of the world were [one] supercontinent now called Pangaea. Sometime around the early Jurassic, the continents we know today began to separate. Florida, originally part of the African plate, was left behind as a part of North America. For the next 140 million years, Florida was underwater.

"Although dinosaurs never lived in Florida, when it comes to fossils from the Age of Mammals, Florida is probably the richest state east of the Mississippi. The oldest surface rocks are about 50 million years old and contain mainly invertebrate fossils that lived in these ancient Florida seas. One occasionally finds vertebrate fossils in the limestone: bones and teeth from sharks, bony fish, whales, dolphins, walruses, and seacows.

"Between 24 million and 5 million years ago, in the Miocene Epoch, land animals occupied most of present-day Florida, with the exception of some coastal areas and much of south Florida, which remained underwater. Animals from this period include three-toed horses, primitive cats, hyena-like dogs, giant bear-dogs (*Amphicyon*), rhinos, gomphotheres (elephant relatives that possessed both upper and lower tusks), camels (including *Epicamelus*, a giraffe-sized camel),

alligators, crocodiles, giant tortoises, peccaries, otters, and many strange-looking, antelope-like animals.

"Miocene fossil-collecting sites are fairly common in Florida. The most famous area is the phosphate-mining region east of Tampa. Miners found so many bones in their search for phosphate that they named the area Bone Valley; geologists later renamed it the Bone Valley Formation. Limestone quarries often contain Miocene fossils. Shark's teeth are common, including those of *Carcharodon megalodon*, the extinct, sixty-foot-long shark, which had teeth eight inches long.

"The Florida fossil record is also extremely rich in animal life from the Pleistocene Epoch, 1.8 million years ago, which saw three major glaciations [periods of time when glaciers were common]. The closest that any glacier came to Florida was the Ohio River Valley, 700 miles away. But even that was enough to make Florida's climate cooler and wetter than today. At the peak of North American glaciation, Florida's land area was almost doubled, and was home to mammoths and mastodons, saber-toothed tigers and cave bears, dire wolves, giant ground sloths, and many other animals, some of which are still here today."

WALT DISNEY WORLD RESORT

Walt Disney World is not just an amusement park. Its Epcot Center has a Future World attraction called "Universe of Energy" that takes visitors back in time to an ancient dinosaur habitat. It's complete with Disney's famous Audio Animatronic versions of *Apatosaurus*, *Stegosaurus*, *Allosaurus*, and other prehistoric creatures. Special effects attempt to reproduce weather conditions, as well as an active volcano. The "smellitzer machine" even injects the visitors' environment with scents designed to heighten the reality of the ride.

P.O. Box 10040
Lake Buena Vista, FL
  32830-0040
(407) 824-4321

Admission: High fee

Facilities: Rest rooms, gift shops, food available, wheelchair accessible

MULBERRY PHOSPHATE FOSSIL MUSEUM

Workers mining phosphate, a mineral used for soap and other things, came across a rich trove of fossils near here. This museum offers a closer look at these wonderful "leftovers" of Florida's mining industry.

P.O. Box 707
Mulberry, FL 33860
(813) 425-2823

Admission: Low fee

Facilities: Rest rooms, gift shop, wheelchair accessible

THE CONSERVANCY NATURE CENTER

At this nature center, Florida's prehistory is illustrated in three separate dioramas and a respectable group of fossil plants, animals, and shells. Other important facts about Florida's natural resources are explored in a group of conservation-centered exhibits.

1450 Merrihue Drive
Naples, FL 33942
(813) 262-0304

Admission: Donation requested

Facilities: Rest rooms, gift shop

UNIVERSAL STUDIOS FLORIDA

The "Back to the Future" thrill ride at this amusement park takes you directly into the jaws of a hungry *Tyrannosaurus rex*—or so it seems. But the real dinosaur excitement comes via the new "Jurassic Park" ride, exhibit, and shop, unveiled early in 1994. Modeled after the movie of the same name, it combines fact and fiction, with motion-picture monsters and real fossils both displayed. And if that isn't enough, fans of cartoon prehistory can take the "Fantastic World of Hanna-Barbera" ride to good old Bedrock, home of the Flintstones.

1000 Universal Studio
  Plaza
Orlando, FL
  32819-7610
(407) 824-4321

Admission: Moderate fee

Facilities: Rest rooms, gift shops, food available, wheelchair accessible

JUNIOR MUSEUM OF BAY COUNTY

This museum was designed for kids of all ages, with hands-on exhibits that visitors are encouraged to touch and fully experience. Included are prehistoric fossils from Florida and nearby locales.

1731 Jenks Avenue
Panama City, FL 32405
(904) 769-6128

Admission: Low fee

Facilities: Rest rooms, gift shop, wheelchair accessible

MUSEUM OF FLORIDA HISTORY

A prehistoric mastodon twelve feet tall is the "high point" of this museum's paleo resources. Florida's state history is also covered, from the time of the Spanish explorers to modern days.

R. A. Gray Building
500 South Bronough
  Street
Tallahassee, FL
  32399-0250
(904) 769-6128

Admission: Low fee

Facilities: Rest rooms, gift shop

Archidiskodon

CURATOR'S CORNER

DR. S. DAVID WEBB

Florida State Museum, University of Florida,
Love Bone Bed

"We Florida paleontologists try to arrange our field seasons for the cooler months of the year, and certainly not for August," says Dr. Webb. "But during that month, in the summer of 1974, I received a call from a farmer named Ron Love about a very [thick, heavy] iron-stained bone that didn't look "normal." He was right. It was the tibia [foreleg bone] of a short-legged rhinoceros, extinct for at least 4 million years. He and I both became rather excited about it.

"The next day, despite the high temperatures and humidity, found us digging between the rows of okra plants where he had [dug] up the tibia and some other bone fragments. A month later, all able hands from my laboratory had wrecked about five percent of Ron Love's okra crop, with much help and encouragement from him. That was the genesis of my favorite fossil site, the Love Bone Bed.

"Over the years, we worked with hand tools and wheelbarrows until the overburden [dirt covering the fossil bed] became too deep. Then I would rent a back-hoe to remove the overburden and to dig long, deep test trenches. Ron Love had leased us that acre and moved his crops. Eventually we outlined the shape of an ancient stream channel . . . nearly thirty feet below the original surface.

"*Barbourofelis lovei* [a "false" saber cat found in the stream channel] was new to science, [so] we named it after the landowner. Not only did we find its skull, but scattered through the site were many examples of [nearly] all of its skeletal parts. That is how our museum became the first to mount a whole skeleton. Anyone could see the imbalance between its weaker hind limbs and its massive forelimbs. It could not have been much of a runner, but instead was an ambush cat, relying on its powerful saber teeth and forelimbs."

GEORGIA

FERNBANK MUSEUM OF NATURAL HISTORY

 A twenty-foot *Albertosaurus* model encircled by models of other dinosaurs and an elaborate dinosaur mural are highlights of this museum's Dinosaur Room. But don't miss the specialized kids' activity centers: "Georgia Adventure," for children six to ten years old, and the "Fantasy Forest" for kids three to five.

767 Clifton Road N.E.
Atlanta, GA 30307
(404) 378-0127

Admission: Low fee

Facilities: Rest rooms, gift shop, food available, wheelchair accessible

---

CURATOR'S CORNER

DAVID SCHWIMMER

Paleontologist
Columbus College School of Science

"When I arrived in Georgia fifteen years ago to teach paleontology, I wasn't sure there would be much to work with," Dr. Schwimmer remembers. "No dinosaur fossils had ever been found in the state. I began asking everyone in the region if they had ever seen fossil bones or teeth.

"Over the next two years, I examined a huge collection—of junk. Until one day, a local hunter brought a gathering of shark's teeth (which are common), crocodile teeth (less common), and a heavy bone scrap that may or may not have been from a dinosaur. It was water-tumbled and pretty much unidentifiable. He showed me to the spot where he'd gathered this collection, and over fifteen years I have collected evidence of three species of dinosaur, plus crocodiles, mosasaurs, plesiosaurs, more than thirty types of fish, turtles, and a huge assortment of invertebrates from that locality. It is one of the richest fossil sites in the Southeast, although all of the dinosaur bones are just fragments."

FERNBANK SCIENCE CENTER

Only *Struthiomimus*, an ostrich-like donosaur, and a *T. rex* skull and pterosaurs are featured at this hands-on science center created especially for families with kids. Some say it has lost its luster since the newer Fernbank Museum of Natural History opened. But it is still a trusted old friend to many Georgia dinosaur fans.

156 Heaton Park Drive
Atlanta, GA 30307
(404) 378-4311

Admission: Low fee

Facilities: Rest rooms, gift shop, wheelchair accessible

LANIER MUSEUM OF NATURAL HISTORY

A recently restored, three-foot-long scale model of a hadrosaur is just one of several fine dinosaur resources on display at this museum. Trace fossils as well as a *Triceratops* horn and dinosaur tracks are other unique features.

2601 Buford Dam Road
Buford, GA 30518
(404) 932-4460

Admission: Donation requested

Facilities: Rest rooms, gift shop, wheelchair accessible

WEINMAN MINERAL MUSEUM

Though this is primarily a geology museum with a local focus, there are still a few fossils on display including crynoids, trilobites, ancient marine fossils, and microfossils. A few dinosaur tracks are also in this collection.

P.O. Box 1255
Cartersville, GA 30120
(404) 386-0576

Admission: Low fee

Facilities: Rest rooms, gift shop

ROCK EAGLE MUSEUM OF NATURAL HISTORY

Considered a museum with a focus on natural history in general, Rock Eagle has some excellent dinosaur/prehistoric exhibits, thanks in large part to artist and exhibit designer Rick Spears, who created all the illustrations in Part Three of this book. His full-size sixteen-foot-long mosasaur reconstruction model is a lifelike guard at the museum's main entrance. The three-quarters-scale *Albertosaurus* mother feeding her hatchlings was also created by Spears. But don't miss the other enjoyable exhibits, such as an enormous shark, its jaws open wide for curious little visitors to crawl through. (See Curator's Corner.)

Rock Eagle 4-H Center
350 Rock Eagle Road N.W.
Eatonton, GA 31024
(706) 485-2831

Admission: Low fee

Facilities: Rest rooms, gift shop, wheelchair accessible

THE MUSEUM OF ARTS & SCIENCES

 "Ziggy" is the nickname given this museum's eighteen-foot reconstruction of an ancient whale. But scientists know it as *Zygorhiza*. Smaller, fossilized marine animals are also on display.

4182 Forsyth Road
Macon, GA 31210
(912) 477-3232

Admission: Low fee

Facilities: Rest rooms, gift shop, wheelchair accessible

SAVANNAH SCIENCE MUSEUM

Fossils from the Cenozoic Era, along with a full-size mounted skeletal replica of a ground sloth rising up on its hind legs, are this museum's primary paleontological offerings.

4405 Paulsen Street
Savannah, GA 31499
(912) 355-6705

Admission: Low fee

Facilities: Rest rooms, gift shop

CURATOR'S CORNER

RICK SPEARS

Artist/Exhibit Design/Coordinator
Rock Eagle Museum of Natural History

"As a kid, I loved dinosaurs. I knew the names of the dinosaurs better than my multiplication tables! I would draw prehistoric animals and put together plastic models of them, all the time. But as a teenager I got interested in other things and kind of forgot about dinosaurs.

"In my first job after college, I was given a chance to draw dinosaurs for some advertisements. To do a good job, I studied books on dinosaurs. I was surprised that so much new stuff had been written in ten years. The more I read, the more I got interested in dinosaurs again. I began practicing making

my own models, and got pretty good at it. I even started to make models for some museums to use in their exhibits.

"Now I work as a full-time exhibit designer and modelmaker for the Rock Eagle Museum of Natural History. Sometimes I look at pictures of the first models I made several years ago, and they look kind of silly. That's because I've kept studying and practicing, and now I can make more accurate, realistic models. I guess just about everybody likes dinosaurs when they are kids. Unfortunately, a lot of people grow out of it. I'm very happy I grew back into it."

GEORGIA SOUTHERN UNIVERSITY MUSEUM

Don't miss this museum's twenty-seven-foot mosasaur skeleton from South Dakota, or its proud work in progress—the oldest known Vogle whale ever found. A full array of fossils, including a large meteorite found near Statesboro, is also on display. A dinosaur-identification section and a simulated fossil dig are just two of several exhibits created especially for kids.

U.S. 301
Statesboro, GA 30458
(912) 681-5444

Admission: Donation requested

Facilities: Rest rooms, gift shop, wheelchair accessible

Mosasaur

HAWAII

PARADISE PARK

3737 Manoa Road
Honolulu, HI 96822
(808) 988-0233

Admission: Moderate fee

Facilities: Rest rooms, gift shop, food available, wheelchair accessible

Perhaps Dinamation International chose Honolulu as home base for the herd of animated robotic dinosaurs you'll find here because the island has no dinosaur fossil native to the area—the land itself is far too young for most prehistoric animals. Maybe they decided to plant their model reconstructions in Hawaii because it is already a popular vacation spot. But whatever the reason, Paradise Park, once a home for tropical birds and plants, became a prehistoric nature reserve before *Jurassic Park* was filmed in Hawaii.

JURASSIC PARK MOVIE LOCATION

c/o Kauai Film
  Commission
4444 Rice Street,
  Room 204
Lihue, Kauai, HI 96766
(808) 241-6390

Admission: High fee

Facilities: None

Although much of *Jurassic Park* was actually filmed in Hollywood, some amazing locations were shot on private property in Kauai, and you can see the same views via helicopter tour. Call the Kauai Film Commission to arrange the trip. Steven Spielberg also used the same general area years before for a tropical backdrop in *Raiders of the Lost Ark*.

NATIONAL TROPICAL BOTANICAL GARDENS

P.O. Box 340
Lawai, HI 96765
(808) 332-7324

Admission: Low fee

Facilities: Rest rooms, gift shop, wheelchair accessible

Another setting used for the film *Jurassic Park*, there are no dinosaurs at these gardens, just the lush, green backdrop for some serious dinosaur movie fun. Even so, don't miss the chance to see it, if you're in Lawai.

IDAHO

HAGERMAN FOSSIL BEDS NATIONAL MONUMENT

 Centuries ago, more than 130 prehistoric species lived at what is now a national monument. Hagerman is considered one of the finest fossil beds in the world, rich with mammals and other prehistoric animals from the Pliocene Period. There is an interpretive center and a staff to explain the fossils to you.

P.O. Box 570
Hagerman, ID 83332
(208) 837-4793

Admission: Low fee

Facilities: Rest rooms, gift shop, wheelchair accessible

IDAHO STATE MUSEUM OF NATURAL HISTORY

Renovations were completed in 1993 to freshen and update this museum's exhibits, including its paleo resources. The exhibits center around an outstanding group of Pleistocene mammals, with *Bison latifrons* featured. Dinosaurs were not a part of Idaho's ancient history, at least not according to the fossil evidence collected thus far. But some dinosaur fossils from other areas will be on display, and new discoveries are being made every day. Idaho paleontologists are hopeful.

Idaho State University
Campus Box 8096
Pocatello, ID
  83209-0009
(208) 236-3168

Admission: Low fee

Facilities: Rest rooms, gift shop, food available, wheelchair accessible

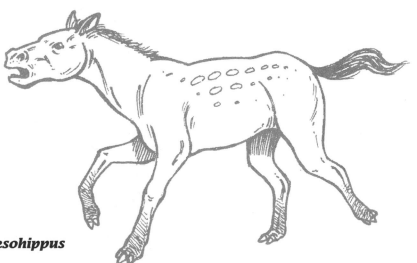

Mesohippus

CURATOR'S CORNER

DR. GREG MCDONALD

Paleontologist
Hagerman Fossil Beds National Monument

"Paleontological research in the Hagerman began in 1929, when Dr. James Gidley of the Smithsonian Institution's National Museum of Natural History visited the area to investigate a report of some fossil horse bones," says Dr. McDonald.

"His visit resulted in four seasons of fieldwork in what is now known as the Hagerman Horse Quarry. During those four seasons, the Smithsonian collected the remains of at least 120 extinct zebralike horses, as well as those of turtles, peccaries, ground sloths, antelope, dirk-toothed cats, and mastodons. Later work showed that the area was also rich in the often overlooked remains of small animals such as mice, shrews, rabbits, fish, frogs, and snakes.

"Today, over 105 different species of fossil animals are known from the Hagerman Fossil Beds."

ILLINOIS

AURORA HISTORICAL MUSEUM

This museum shows bones that one U.S. government work crew found in 1934. They thought these were old cow bones, but in fact they were discovered to be the ancient bones of a mastodon. These bones of an elephant's distant relative are featured along with other exhibits of local history.

317 Ceder Street
Aurora, IL 60506
(708) 897-9029

Admission: Low fee

Facilities: Rest rooms, gift shop, wheelchair accessible

SCI TECH

No regular dinosaur exhibit is featured, but Sci Tech has booked traveling dinosaur exhibits in the past, so call to find out what exhibits might be scheduled during your stay in Aurora.

18 West Benton
Aurora, IL 60506
(708) 859-3434

Admission: Low fee

Facilities: Rest rooms, gift shop, food available

CHICAGO ACADEMY OF SCIENCE

A prehistoric coal forest and an Ice Age cave are two fine examples of what the Chicago Academy of Science has to offer fossil fans. Another feature is the Dinosaur Alcove, an escape for kids of all ages, featuring dinosaur-related games and puzzles.

2001 North Clark Street
Chicago, IL 60614
(312) 871-2668

Admission: Low fee

Facilities: Rest rooms, gift shop, food available, wheelchair accessible

FIELD MUSEUM OF NATURAL HISTORY

The year 1994 marked this world-famous museum's one hundredth birthday! All of its dinosaur mounts and exhibits were dismantled and remodeled to reflect exciting modern discoveries, including a huge *Brachiosaurus*. The latest thinking about *Albertosaurus*, *Lambeosaurus*, *Apatosaurus*, mastodon, mammoth, saber-toothed cat, ground sloth, and other animals' lifestyles will be reflected in the new displays (see Curator's Corner).

Roosevelt Road at Lake Shore Drive
Chicago, IL 60605
(312) 922-9410

Admission: Low fee

Facilities: Rest rooms, gift shop, food available, wheelchair accessible

CURATOR'S CORNER

DR. J. MICHAEL PARRISH

Biological Sciences Department
Northern Illinois University

"In recent years," says Dr. Parrish, "I have done a lot of my 'digging' in museums around the world, as I have tried to help sort out the relationships between dinosaurs, crocodiles, and their nearest relatives, mostly crocodile-like animals that lived around 200 million years ago. This project alone has led me to museums on every continent, except Antarctica and Australia.

"However, the biggest thrills still come from finding and digging up fossils—from being the first person to gaze on the remains of an animal that might have been hidden from view for tens to hundreds of millions of years. Because Illinois is not known for its rich dinosaur beds, I do most of my fieldwork in the Southwest, primarily [in] Arizona, Utah, and Colorado.

"Dinosaur digs aside, Illinois is a great place to be a paleontologist, because it offers huge research collections, some of the world's best libraries, and one of the world's biggest concentrations of paleontologists with whom I can brainstorm."

ELGIN PUBLIC MUSEUM

Fifteen thousand specimens, including fossils and minerals, are displayed at this museum. Outside, 120 acres of park space are also worth a visit.

225 Grand Boulevard
Elgin, IL 60121
(708) 741-6655

Admission: Low fee

Facilities: Rest rooms, gift shop, food available, wheelchair accessible

WESTERN ILLINOIS UNIVERSITY GEOLOGY MUSEUM

A *Protoceratops* nest with eggs is the highlight of the dinosaur exhibit at this geology museum. Two other museums on campus also welcome visitors: the American History Museum and the Greenhouse Museum (the latter is devoted to plants and gardening).

Macomb, IL 61455
(309) 298-1151, or
 (309) 298-1368

Admission: Donation requested

Facilities: Rest rooms, wheelchair accessible

FUNK ROCK & MINERAL MUSEUM

 Fossils are featured in only one part of this museum, but the general rock and mineral collection is impressive.

Route 1
Shirley, IL 61772
(309) 827-6792

Admission: Low fee

Facilities: Rest rooms, gift shop, food available, wheelchair accessible

ILLINOIS STATE MUSEUM

 One of the world's largest mastodon skeletons towers over visitors at the Illinois State Museum. Kids of all ages can dig for fossils in the museum's "Discovery Place"—a room full of hands-on natural history exhibits.

Spring and Edward Streets
Springfield, IL 62706
(217) 782-7386

Admission: Donation requested

Facilities: Rest rooms, gift shop, wheelchair accessible

LAKEVIEW MUSEUM OF ARTS AND SCIENCES

 The largest museum in western Illinois, Lakeview has a wealth of fossils and ancient bones, but its planetarium is still the popular favorite.

1125 West Lake Avenue
Peoria, IL 61650
(309) 686-7000

Admission: Low fee

Facilities: Rest rooms, gift shop, wheelchair accessible

THE FRYXELL GEOLOGY MUSEUM

 From the oldest and tiniest fossils (including single-celled algae dating back 2 billion years) to trilobites, dinosaurs, and mammoths, the Fryxell Geology Museum houses a remarkable variety of prehistoric fossils, but all aspects of geology are explored.

New Science Building
Augustana College
Rock Island, IL 61201
(309) 794-8513

Admission: Low fee

Facilities: Rest rooms, gift shop, wheelchair accessible

CURATOR'S CORNER

WILLIAM F. SIMPSON

Chief Preparator and Collections Manager
of Fossil Vertebrates, Department of Geology
Field Museum of Natural History

Speaking of the remodeling of his museum's Dinosaur Hall, Mr. Simpson says, "All of our skeletons were recently moved from the old hall to the new hall, and many, including dinosaurs such as *Apatosaurus*, were remounted in more lifelike poses. It was my job to make sure the fossil bones were handled properly and not broken during the whole process. When the new exhibit opened in the summer of 1994, 'my bones' looked even more exciting than when I first saw them years ago!

"Another exciting exhibit just opened in 1994—the mounting of the gigantic *Brachiosaurus* skeleton. We have had the skeleton for which the dinosaur was named since 1900, when the Field Museum dug up the bones in Colorado. But this is a very incomplete skeleton and a little hard to understand without more bones. We finally decided to erect a complete fiberglass copy of a *Brachiosaurus* so that people would understand what they were looking at when they saw the real bones on display next to it. Again, it was my job to look out for the safety of the real fossils. I supervised the restoration and the molding of the bones. The missing portion of the skeleton was based on a more complete *Brachiosaurus altithorax* found by the Germans in Africa.

INDIANA

INDIANA UNIVERSITY–PURDUE UNIVERSITY AT FORT WAYNE GEOLOGY MUSEUM

 A group of Ice Age mammals are on exhibit at this campus museum, although prehistory is only one of many themes explored. The well-known paleontologist Dr. James O. Farlow is on staff at Purdue. If you've seen a dinosaur program on public television, you've probably seen Dr. Farlow (see Curator's Corner).

2101 Coliseum
  Boulevard East
Fort Wayne, IN
  46805-1499
(219) 481-6100

Admission: Free

Facilities: Rest rooms, gift shop, food available, wheelchair accessible

CHILDREN'S MUSEUM OF INDIANAPOLIS

The museum's mascot is Rex, a playful *Tyrannosaurus*. But just outside the museum is a model of his not so playful cousin, *Tyrannosaurus rex*. Also on display is the skeleton of an Ice Age mastodon and a very small group of dinosaur fossils. Plans are in the works for a more extensive dinosaur exhibit.

3000 North Meridian
  Street
Indianapolis, IN 46208
(317) 924-5431

Admission: Low fee

Facilities: Rest rooms, gift shop, food available, wheelchair accessible

INDIANA STATE MUSEUM

See 450-million-year-old fossils at this Indiana museum, plus what some area scientists consider a good cross-section of Ice Age mammal fossil evidence.

202 North Alabama
  Street
Indianapolis, IN 46204
(317) 232-1637

Admission: Low fee

Facilities: Rest rooms, gift shop, wheelchair accessible

FALLS OF THE OHIO STATE PARK

Marine invertebrate fossils 350 million years old can be found at this state park, but they are easier to see at certain times of the day and certain times of the year, because of the natural lighting. These fossil beds are said to be some of the oldest in the world. The 16,000-square-foot interpretive center, with exhibits, opened in late 1993. Here you'll find maps and instructions on how to see the outdoor fossils.

914 East Main Street
New Albany, IN 47150
(812) 945-6284

Admission: Low fee

Facilities: Rest rooms, gift shop, wheelchair accessible

JOSEPH MOORE MUSEUM OF NATURAL HISTORY

The most famous fossil in this museum is a bear-sized beaver rescued from a fire in 1924 by a brave student who broke into the science lab, wrestled the giant fossil onto his back, and carried it to safety. Other prehistoric mammals are also displayed.

Earlham College
National Road West
Richmond, IN 47374
(317) 983-1303

Admission: Low fee

Facilities: Rest rooms, gift shop, wheelchair accessible

Epigaulus hatcheri

CURATOR'S CORNER

DR. JAMES O. FARLOW

Professor of Geology
Indiana University–Purdue University at Fort Wayne

"Perhaps the most memorable moment in my career as a paleontologist occurred the first time I worked on a dinosaur footprint site," Dr. Farlow recollects. "This was in Kimble County, Texas, with a group of students. We were there to measure, map, photograph, and otherwise document the tracks. One afternoon the students were off with another professor. I was at the site by myself, making casts of individual footprints to take back to the lab.

"It was a beautiful sunny day. There wasn't a sound of another person—just the scraping of my boots as I walked around the site, and the sloshing of water as I mixed plaster. But there were other sounds aplenty—the soft sighing of the wind through scrub vegetation, the occasional cry of a hawk.

"And there was lots of movement in my vicinity. Numerous small lizards scuttered about, scampering from rock to bush, occasionally stopping to cock their little heads and give me speculative looks. I didn't bother to chase them, and just went about my business, greasing the dinosaur tracks and pouring plaster batter into them. One of the lizards, though, darted from under my feet and came to a stop on the lip of a splendid theropod footprint. And there it stayed, looking over the rim of the track at me: tiny modern reptile, seeking refuge in a step taken by a much larger, far-distant kinsman, more than a hundred million years ago. What a demonstration of the changed fortunes of the reptiles since the end of the Cretaceous!"

IOWA

IOWA HISTORICAL MUSEUM

Iowa fossils, including many collected by Amel Priest and his mentor, Dr. Burnice Beane (see Curator's Corner), are part of this museum's exhibits highlighting state history and prehistory. Some of the world's most impressive crinoids—sea-lily-like animals that predate the dinosaurs—are from Iowa.

600 East Locust Street
Des Moines, IA 50309
(515) 281-5111

Admission: Low fee

Facilities: Rest rooms, gift shop, wheelchair accessible

UNIVERSITY OF IOWA MUSEUM OF NATURAL HISTORY

Iowa was underwater during the time of the dinosaurs, so the fossil record is rich in invertebrate fossil materials such as crinoids and starfish. But Ice Age mammals were very much a part of Iowa's prehistory, and are exhibited along with the sea creatures in this university museum. Included is a giant ground sloth nine feet tall.

Iowa City, IA 52242
(319) 335-0480

Admission: Donation requested

Facilities: Rest rooms, gift shop, food available, wheelchair accessible

---

CURATOR'S CORNER

AMEL PRIEST

private fossil collector

"There have been several important finds of crinoids in Iowa. After collecting at Gilmore City one day, I stopped at a small quarry just south of the big one. Someone had just set off a blast right through the middle of a nest of crinoids. You'd better believe I went back the next day. It turned out to be my most memorable fossil find. They had just blasted right down through a nest of *Cactocrinus imperator*. Slabs were just covered with entwining columns and crowns of this lovely and impressive crinoid. There were a dozen or more openly displayed crowns, with many others partly hidden. It was really exciting to turn over a large slab plastered with such a display."

CORALVILLE LAKE SPILLWAY

When the Coalville dam failed in the flood of 1993, a wall of water cut a gorge through this spillway, exposing fossils from the Devonian Period of the Paleozoic Era—some 350 million years ago. Plans are afoot to construct an interpretive center, but you can see the site now if you call the ranger station for directions, and there is a stand on site with brochures that describe the fossils. More than 75,000 people had visited the new fossil find within two months after the floodwaters receded.

2850 Prairie Duchien Road
Iowa City, IA 52240
(319) 338-3543
  (ranger station)

Admission: No fee

Facilities: None

MADISON COUNTY HISTORICAL COMPLEX

When eighty-five-year-old Amel Priest decided to give away his huge collection of Iowa fossils, three museums offered to house them: Washington, D.C.'s Smithsonian Institution, the state of Iowa's geology experts at the Iowa Historical Museum, and this county museum. Because Mr. Priest had lived in Madison County for so many years, he decided to give his collection to this local historical complex. Consisting largely of invertebrate fossils, it is considered one of Iowa's best collections. Crinoids are beautiful, ancient, plantlike animals, much like modern sea lilies. Dr. Beane and Mr. Priest spent decades searching for these and other Iowa invertebrate fossils.

815 South Second Avenue
Winterset, IA 50273
(515) 462-2134

Admission: Low fee

Facilities: Rest rooms, gift shop, food available

CURATOR'S CORNER

RALPH A. BEANE

son of the noted fossil collector,
Dr. Burnice H. Beane

"Without a doubt, my father's greatest discovery was made in the summer of 1931. After a blast in the Le Grand quarry, he was searching for crinoids and came across a slab of rock about three by five feet, containing some fossil starfish. With the aid of some of the quarry workers, they got the 650-pound slab loaded on a truck and [my father] took it home. After removing a thin layer of stone, he found that it contained 183 near-perfect starfish, twelve sea urchins, two blastoids, and a number of other [early] marine animals. Dr. Schukert of Yale University, an authority on fossil starfish, claimed that it was the greatest starfish slab ever found. It is on display at the Iowa Historical Museum in Des Moines.

"Some forty different species of fossil crinoids have been found in the Le Grand quarry. In 1937 my father was invited to collaborate with Dr. Lowell R. Lowden of Tulsa University on a study of Le Grand crinoids, and to publish a comprehensive description of all the local species. He was given the additional honor of naming eleven new species in recognition of local friends. One species was named for George F. Kirby, the owner of the Le Grand quarry, who had enabled [my father] to enjoy his lifelong hobby.

"Dr. Burnice H. Beane passed away on January 15, 1966, at the age of eighty-six. Just a year before his death, a new species was named for him. The scientific name is *Rhodocrinites beanei*. I am proud of my father for his achievements. Some specimens from his collection can be found in many universities and museums, in the United States and in several foreign countries."

KANSAS

THE PIONEER MUSEUM

 At this museum, you can see a rare collection of prehistoric animal bones all found locally in Ashland, including mammals and marine life.

U.S. Route 160
Ashland, KS 67031
(316) 635-2227

Admission: Low fee

Facilities: Rest rooms, gift shop

KANSAS OIL MUSEUM

 This museum traces five hundred years of the history of oil (which comes from fossils) in Kansas. Don't expect anything focused specifically on dinosaurs, but the exhibit is worth stretching your legs to explore.

383 East Central
El Dorado, KS 67042
(316) 321-9333

Admission: Free

Facilities: Rest rooms

STERNBERG MEMORIAL MUSEUM

This medium-sized museum, named for one of the early twentieth century's most famous amateur fossil hunters, has a fossil collection worth seeing. The fish-within-a-fish fossil features the fierce ocean giant *Xiphactinus* and the lunch it swallowed moments before death. But most of Kansas was underwater during dino days, so dinosaurs are rare. Most exhibits feature marine life, pterosaurs, and Kansas prehistory, including early bison, camels, horses, rhinos, and oxen, as well as mammoths, mastodons, and ground sloths.

Fort Hayes State
  University
600 Park
Hays, KS 67601
(913) 628-4286

Admission: Low fee

Facilities: Rest rooms, gift shop, food available

CURATOR'S CORNER

SHIRLEY ADE

Museum Director
McPherson Museum

"The medium-sized ground sloth in our display stood a little over six feet tall and weighed about 3,000 pounds," says Ms. Ade. "Its simple, peglike teeth indicate that it probably preferred a diet of grass, although it may also have fed on tubers, bushes, and trees. Ground sloths were primitive animals related to present-day armadillos and the small tree sloths of Central and South America. [The specimen was taken from the La Brea Tar Pits in Los Angeles, California.] The other skeleton we have from the La Brea Pits is the dire wolf.

"The preservation of these fossils is an interesting process. Asphalt seeped to the surface through ancient stream channel deposits. The resulting puddles were often concealed by a surface coating of leaves and dust or water. Occasionally an unwary animal became trapped in the asphalt. Its cries alerted predators and scavengers that were lured in and also became trapped. After the animals died, the bodies soon decayed and the individual bones became saturated with asphalt and settled into the mire. In the summer months, the hot asphalt became mobile and moved the bones around—causing them to be mixed with other bones. Because of this phenomenon, there are very few complete skeletons recovered from Rancho La Brea. [Our skeletons] are composites of several different skeletons."

DYCHE MUSEUM OF NATURAL HISTORY

Ankylosaurs and hadrosaurs were native to Kansas, and are the only dinosaurs found in the state, so far. Fossils from such marine animals as ichthyosaurs and huge, prehistoric sea turtles make up the most of this museum's fossil resources. One of the largest pterosaur fossils ever found is on display here—a *Pteranodon* with a twenty-five-foot wingspan. And don't miss Comanche, a stuffed and mounted U.S. cavalry horse—the only surviving "soldier" from the Battle of the Little Big Horn. Dr. Larry Martin, an expert on prehistoric birds, who is often featured on dinosaur documentaries, is the curator of paleontology.

University of Kansas
Jayhawk Boulevard
Lawrence, KS
(913) 864-4540

Admission: Donation requested

Facilities: Rest rooms, food available

MCPHERSON MUSEUM

Like other Kansas museums, McPherson has fossils of Ice Age mammals, including a giant ground sloth and a saber-tooth cat. Again, dinosaur discoveries are rare in Kansas, because much of the state was underwater in their time.

1130 East Euclid
McPherson, KS 67460
(316) 241-3340, or
  (316) 241-5977

Admission: Low fee

Facilities: Rest rooms, gift shop

FICK FOSSIL MUSEUM

Where else could you find 11,000 fossils and specimens of prehistoric sharks' teeth, fossil art, and much more material on the geologic history of Kansas? This museum is small but worth the stop. A rare fossil fish known as *Portheus molossus*, fifteen feet long, is one of the museum's prized specimens. Monument Rocks, the first National Natural Landmark established in Kansas, is only twenty-six miles south of Oakley

700 West Third
Oakley, KS 67748
(913) 672-4839

Admission: Low fee

Facilities: Rest rooms, gift shop

GRANT COUNTY MUSEUM

This museum houses a pair of mastodon tusks as the best of its fossil collection. But its main focus is on local history rather than on paleontology.

300 East U.S.
  Route 160
Ulysses, KS 67880
(316) 356-3009

Admission: Donation requested

Facilities: Rest rooms

Ground sloth

KENTUCKY

NORTHEASTERN KENTUCKY HISTORY MUSEUM

 A small collection of prehistoric fossils is included at this museum of Kentucky state history.

State Route 182
Carter Caves, KY 41128
(606) 286-6012

Admission: Donation requested

Facilities: Rest rooms, wheelchair accessible

BEHRINGER-CRAWFORD MUSEUM

Fossils excavated from the Big Bone Lick site are on display at this museum. Most of Big Bone Lick State Park's (see below) educational programs originate from Behringer-Crawford, as a cooperative effort.

Devou Park
P.O. Box 677
1600 Montague Avenue
Covington, KY
 41012-0067
(606) 491-4003

Admission: Low fee

Facilities: Rest rooms, gift shop, wheelchair accessible

LEXINGTON CHILDREN'S MUSEUM

Fossil exhibits include a dig to discover an *Archaeopteryx* cast, a "put the bones together" puzzle, a puzzle using trilobites to establish a sequence of strata, an activity box to distinguish fossils from pseudofossils and another one for identification of "coal swamp" fossils. Both the activity boxes use locally collected fossils. There are also hands-on fossils for simple examination.

401 West Main Street
Lexington, KY 40505
606 258-3253

Admission: Low fee

Facilities: Rest rooms, gift shop, wheelchair accessible

BLUE LICKS BATTLEFIELD STATE PARK

 American history is the focus of this state park and museum; the last official battle of the Revolutionary War was allegedly fought at this location. But the soldiers were fighting on the death site of mastodons and other Ice Age mammals. Some prehistoric finds are on display at the museum.

P.O. Box 66
Mount Olivet, KY
 41064-0066
(606) 289-5507

Admission: Low fee

Facilities: Rest rooms, gift shop

CURATOR'S CORNER

ROBERT D. LINDY

Park Manager
Big Bone Lick State Park

"In prehistoric times, great herds of giant mastodons, mammoths, bison, primitive horses, and sloths lived in this area of north-central Kentucky," says Mr. Lindy. "The huge beasts, attracted to the salt found in abundance in the swampland, [got stuck] in the ooze and died.

"When the American Indians guided the French explorer [Charles Le Moyne, baron] de Longueuil to Big Bone Lick in 1739, bones were lying on the marshy ground. By 1840, it was estimated that the bones of hundreds of mammals had been removed from the area, which today has many bones and research materials displayed in the museum. The warm salt springs are still visible.

"Visitors are introduced to the fascinating history of Big Bone Lick in a museum with displays of ancient bones and a video presentation about the history of Big Bone Lick. An outdoor museum contains life-size models of the prehistoric mastodon and bison, the last remaining salt-sulfur spring, and a model 'dig' containing bone samples and replicas. A live herd of [modern] buffalo [is] on permanent display."

OWENSBORO AREA MUSEUM

This museum houses exhibits on paleontology and archaeology that reflect local history.

Griffith and College
  Streets
Owensboro, KY 42302
(502) 683-0296

Admission: Low fee

Facilities: Rest rooms, wheelchair accessible

BIG BONE LICK STATE PARK

Prehistoric mammals met their deaths at what is now a state park, but was once a salty, sticky swamp. Their fossilized skeletal remains were retrieved and distributed to museums worldwide. The visitor center/museum offers a video explanation of the park's history. Models of some of the ancient victims are on display outside, along with a replica of a paleontological dig. Many of the fossils are being held in trust until funds can be raised to properly display and care for them at the state park.

3380 Beaver Road
Union, KY 41091
(606) 384-3522

Admission: Low fee

Facilities: Rest rooms, gift shop, wheelchair accessible

LOUISIANA

LAFAYETTE MUSEUM OF NATURAL HISTORY

A major dinosaur exhibit is scheduled to open at the museum in the near future, and traveling exhibits are often featured. Call to check on scheduled exhibits if you plan a stop in or near Lafayette.

(until new exhibit opens)

637 Gerard Park Drive
Lafayette, LA 70502
(318) 234-2208

Admission: Low fee

Facilities: Rest rooms, gift shop, wheelchair accessible

AUDUBON INSTITUTE-PATHWAYS TO THE PAST

Although the Audubon Institute is well known for its zoo, the recently built Pathways to the Past—a natural history museum on the zoo grounds—is devoted entirely to exploring the dinosaur/bird connection. Four distinctive exhibits on locomotion, reproduction, ancestry, temperatures/climates, and a lifelike *Coelophysis* model reconstruction and diorama are housed within a circular building, along with related "hands-on" learning centers. The museum was designed with young people in mind, but this is an outstanding opportunity for visitors of all ages.

6500 Magazine Street
New Orleans, LA 70118
(504) 861-2537

Admission: Low fee

Facilities: Rest rooms, gift shop, food available, wheelchair accessible

MUSEUM OF NATURAL HISTORY
NORTHEAST LOUISIANA UNIVERSITY

Fossils and exhibits on paleontology and archaeology are small and nestled among other historic materials at this museum. But it's a great place to stretch your legs and explore, even if the paleo resources are limited.

Hanna Hall
Monroe, LA 71209
(318) 342-1884

Admission: Donation requested

Facilities: Rest rooms, food available, wheelchair accessible

CURATOR'S CORNER

DR. JUDITH A. SCHIEBOUT

Museum of Natural Science
Louisiana State University

"Louisiana doesn't have extensive, open badlands for fossil hunting, or exposures of terrestrial rocks of the right age to yield dinosaurs," says Dr. Schiebout, "but we do recover some fossil mammals, in part, by counting on the help of people who encounter something unusual. I recall with gratitude the Corps of Engineers, who supported excavation at an Eocene marine site in the center of the state, and helped out by lifting the field cast of a beautiful skull of the primitive whale *Basilosaurus* up a steep bluff on a bulldozer blade. Careful preparation of this specimen in our lab yielded even the tiny inner-ear bones.

"Another lucky find came about when local industry was digging a cooling pond and its bulldozer operator hit bone—a mastodon, an Ice Age elephant relative. He reported the find, and work was halted until the university could excavate."

MAINE

MAINE STATE MUSEUM

 Exhibits here feature Ice Age mammals, including mammoth and mastodon remains and an ancient walrus skull found by a fourteen-year-old clam digger. Exciting new details about the discovery of a woolly mammoth in 1993 should be on display soon. Found by B. Gary Hoyle of the Maine State Museum, it was the first mammoth specimen ever recovered in Maine (see Curator's Corner).

State Street
Capitol Complex
Augusta, ME 04330
(207) 289-2301

Admission: Low fee

Facilities: Rest rooms, gift shop, food available, wheelchair accessible

CHILDREN'S MUSEUM OF MAINE

 Recently relocated to this new location, the museum has two distinct fossil exhibits. One consists of a collection of tiles imprinted with fossil replicas to study and compare. The other is a conventional museum display featuring prehistoric animal fossils.

142 Free Street
P.O. Box 4041
Portland, ME 04101
(207) 828-1234

Admission: Low fee

Facilities: Rest rooms, gift shop, wheelchair accessible

Mammoth

CURATOR'S CORNER

B. GARY HOYLE

Curator of Natural History
Maine State University

"I have just finished the final fieldwork on the first discovery of a woolly mammoth in Maine," Mr. Hoyle says. "It's been a fascinating project not only because it [proves this ancient elephant lived in more locations than we thought], but, like all good scientific investigations, it generates important questions.

"Because of [years] of water erosion and the scouring action of ancient continental glaciers, all traces of dinosaurs and early vertebrates have been stripped from the landmass of Maine. Nevertheless, about 13,000 years ago, while the last glacier was retreating, the remains of a few vertebrates became trapped in the sediment released by melting ice.

"There is a long-held theory that the enormous weight of the mile-thick glacier [pushed] the land below sea level, then melted away faster than the land could bounce back. Consequently, ocean water followed the retreating glacier many miles inland and covered much of the state of Maine for up to a thousand years.

"However, the discovery of the mammoth bones in clay containing sea shells tells us that the story of Maine's postglacial environment was not so simple. The woolly mammoth was a grazer of grasslands. Where were the grasslands in Maine at that time? How did this creature, which we've nicknamed 'Hairy-it,' die? Did humans butcher it? Were humans even in Maine at that time? We hope that further research at the Maine State Museum will answer some of these questions."

MARYLAND

PEALE MUSEUM

Founded in 1814, this is one of the oldest museums in the United States. Don't miss special exhibits that center on Ice Age mammals. There is not a great deal of fossil material on display, but seeing a historic museum that features some prehistoric animals is worth the stop.

225 Holiday Street
Baltimore, MD 21202
(410) 396-3523

Admission: Low fee

Facilities: Rest rooms, gift shop, food available, wheelchair accessible

CALVERT CLIFFS STATE PARK

The trail to the beach at this state park is a little tricky, but once you get there, you can search for and collect Miocene fossils 10 to 15 million years old. Go to the Merkle ranger's station to pick up maps and instructions. Most of what you'll find will be ancient shells and sharks' teeth. But what you find, you can keep. That is rarely allowed. In fact, unless you have a permit (ordinarily issued to professional experts only), it is illegal to remove most fossils from state or federal land. (See Curator's Corner.)

c/o Merkle Wildlife
  Sanctuary
11704 Fenno Road
Upper Marlboro, MD
  20772
(301) 888-1410

Admission: Free

Facilities: None

CALVERT MARINE MUSEUM

This museum, which features maritime history and the natural history of Maryland, is currently expanding its exhibit on marine fossils. "A Window in Time: Maryland in the Miocene" is scheduled for completion in 1995, and will draw from the state's largest collection of 10-to-20-million-year-old marine fossils. Included will be the world's largest known fossil birds—*Pelagornia*—whales, porpoises, sea turtles, and the jaws of an ancient great white shark. The museum sponsors the CMM Fossil Club.

P.O. Box 97
Solomons, MD 20688
(410) 326-2042

Admission: Low fee

Facilities: Rest rooms, gift shop, wheelchair accessible

CURATOR'S CORNER

RICHARD A. FISHER

Park Ranger
Calvert Cliffs State Park

According to Mr. Fisher, "The cliffs formed over 15 million years ago, when all of southern Maryland was covered by a warm, shallow sea. As marine creatures died, they fell to the bottom of the sea, where they were covered and preserved in many layers of sediment.

"When the last great ice sheets receded, there was a period of uplift in Middle America. The sea fell to its present level, and the bottom of this shallow sea was exposed. The ancient sea floors are now being carved by the wind and waves into the scenic cliffs we see today.

"Over 600 species of fossil life have been identified from the Cliffs. Most abundant are the various species of sharks, along with shells from the phylum *Mollusca* (oysters, clams, etc.).

"A hike of two miles [can be] taken from the parking lot, along an improved trail, to the cliffs/beach area. Natural wave action brings the fossils onto the beach, where they may be collected and kept."

MASSACHUSETTS

PRATT MUSEUM OF NATURAL HISTORY

Earthbound prehistoric birds left behind hundreds of tracks all along the Connecticut River Valley. The Reverend E. B. Hitchcock, then president of Amherst, put together a collection of the tracks, and from them the Pratt Museum of Natural History was born. Dinosaur fossils other than the tracks include fossilized bones of duckbill *Kritosaurus*, as well as *Triceratops* and *Tyrannosaurus rex* and an early amphibian, *Eryops*.

Amherst College
Amherst, MA 01103
(413) 542-2165, or
  (800) 723-1548

Admission: Low fee

Facilities: Rest rooms, gift shop, food available, wheelchair accessible

MUSEUM OF SCIENCE

This is a smaller museum that often features special traveling events. On permanent display are a full-sized *Tyrannosaurus rex* model and a collection of prehistoric fossils.

Science Park
Boston, MA 02114-1099
(617) 723-2500

Admission: Low fee

Facilities: Rest rooms, gift shop, food available, wheelchair accessible

THE MUSEUM OF COMPARATIVE ZOOLOGY

Unique to this museum's hall of vertebrate paleontology is *Stupendemys*, an ancient turtle native to South America 5 to 6 million years ago. The enormous shell measures just over seven feet long. Also on display is *Latimeria chalumnae*—a coelacanth fish that lived during the age of the dinosaur—believed to be extinct until 1938, when fisherman caught one off the coast of Africa. *Dimetrodon* and *Kronosaurus*—ancient reptiles thought to be directly related to modern mammals—are also on display.

Harvard University
Cambridge, MA 02138
(619) 495-2463

Admission: Low fee

Facilities: Rest rooms, gift shop, food available, wheelchair accessible

WISTARIAHURST MUSEUM

Dinosaur tracks are a unique feature on the outer grounds of this proud old Victorian mansion, now a museum. Call ahead for information about the annual "Dinosaur Days" celebration and related activities. (See Curator's Corner.)

238 Cabot Street
Holyoke, MA 01041
(413) 542-2216

Admission: Low fee

Facilities: Rest rooms, gift shop, wheelchair accessible

C. NASH DINOSAUR MUSEUM

This is as much a gift shop as a museum, according to many visitors, because many of the fossils shown are for sale. But what a place to shop! "Dinosaurland," as the museum was once named, was created by amateur collector Carlton Nash, and he found much of what is on display. A quarry on the museum grounds is not generally open to the public, but if Mr. Nash is around, he sometimes shows it to enthusiastic fossil fans. If you're lucky, he'll reflect on decades of dinosaur-hunting adventures.

Route 116, Amherst
  Road
South Hadley, MA
  01075
(413) 467-9566

Admission: Low fee

Facilities: Rest rooms, gift shop, food available, wheelchair accessible

---

CURATOR'S CORNER

SANDRA CHRISTOFORIDIS

Director
Wistariahurst Museum

"The first time I saw dinosaur tracks, I was about five," Ms. Christoforidis recalls. "My parents took me to Dinosaur State Park in Connecticut. I remember thinking how great it was that dinosaurs lived so close to me. Often, something from the past seems so far away. But to see physical evidence so close really brings the past to the present.

"One of the unique aspects of the tracks at Wistariahurst is that they are from Holyoke. In 1927, Belle Skinner, daughter of William Skinner, a silk manufacturer, decided to renovate the house [that is now Wistariahurst]. Part of the renovation was the construction of a semicircular porte cochere. The red shale flagstone [used to construct the driveway] is imprinted with ripple marks and dinosaur tracks from over 170 million years ago. The stones came from a site a few miles away, along the Connecticut River. Today, it's hard to imagine dinosaurs in Holyoke, but they did live here at one time."

SPRINGFIELD SCIENCE MUSEUM

Hands-on exhibits at this museum allow visitors to touch an authentic dinosaur leg bone, a track cast, and a number of other fossils, skeletons, and models including *Tyrannosaurus rex*, *Stegosaurus*, and *Coelophysis*. Don't miss live snakes in the reptile exhibit.

236 State Street
Springfield, MA 01103
(413) 733-1194

Admission: Low fee

Facilities: Rest rooms, gift shop, wheelchair accessible

DINOSAUR FOOTPRINTS RESERVATION

Tracks or footprints from at least three different species of Triassic dinosaurs can be seen at this location. Although Amherst College president Edward Hitchcock discovered similar tracks first in 1836, a mile away at Smith Ferry, these particular tracks were uncovered by work crews in the 1930s, as they cut roads through the area. Visitors are encouraged to explore the trackway, but call ahead for rules and directions. Anyone caught trying to steal or damage the fossils will be prosecuted. Please help to keep them safe for the future.

c/o The Trustees of Reservations
Western Regional Office
P.O. Box 792
Stockbridge, MA 01261
(413) 298-3239

Admission: Free

Facilities: None

BARTON COVE FOOTPRINT QUARRY

Here you'll find another group of dinosaur tracks in the fossil-rich Connecticut Valley, cared for by conservationists from nearby cities. Write or call the Greenfield County Chamber of Commerce for directions and rules.

Turner's Falls, MA
c/o Greenfield County
  Chamber of Commerce
395 Main Street
Greenfield, MA 01301
(413) 773-5463

Admission: Free

Facilities: None

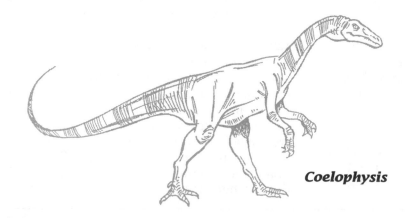

Coelophysis

MICHIGAN

UNIVERSITY OF MICHIGAN EXHIBIT MUSEUM

 This museum's Hall of Evolution is a display of prehistoric life that includes skeletal remains of *Allosaurus*, *Stegosaurus*, *Anatosaurus*, *Tyrannosaurus rex*, and *Apatosaurus*. Not all are full mounts, but it is certainly worth a visit.

1109 Geddes Avenue
Ann Arbor, MI
  48109-1079
(313) 764-0478

Admission: Donation requested

Facilities: Rest rooms, gift shop, food available, wheelchair accessible

KINGMAN MUSEUM OF NATURAL HISTORY

 This museum has a replica of a *Protoceratops* nesting site discovered in Asia by the famed dinosaur hunter Roy Chapman Andrews. It includes real fossilized eggs and eggshells as well as an adult *Protoceratops* skull and a cast of a tiny *Protoceratops* hatchling. (See Curator's Corner.)

175 Limit Street
Battle Creek, MI 49107
(616) 965-5117

Admission: Low fee

Facilities: Rest rooms, gift shop, wheelchair accessible

CRANBROOK INSTITUTE OF SCIENCE

 The exhibit here is small, as far as dinosaur exhibits go; there are a few dinosaur tracks as well as a nice Ice Age mammal group. But a life-size fiberglass reconstruction model of a *Stegosaurus* stands just outside the main entrance.

500 Lone Pine Road
P.O. Box 801
Bloomfield Hills, MI
  48013
(313) 645-3200

Admission: Low fee

Facilities: Rest rooms, gift shop, wheelchair accessible

KALAMAZOO PUBLIC MUSEUM

Part of a mastodon found just miles from Kalamazoo is on display at this small museum of local history. Other prehistoric offerings include a group of local fossils arranged as a puzzle; kids and adults can match each fossil to its place of origin.

315 South Rose Street
Kalamazoo, MI 49007
(606) 345-7092

Admission: Low fee

Facilities: Rest rooms, gift shop, wheelchair accessible

CURATOR'S CORNER

ROBERT LEARNER

Director
Kingman Museum of Natural History

"Kingman Museum of Natural History's *Protoceratops* exhibit contains a replica of a nest, actual eggs, and eggshells, a cast of a newly hatched baby *Protoceratops*, and the fossilized skull of an adult *Protoceratops*," says Mr. Learner. "These are from a 1922 Gobi Desert expedition by Roy Chapman Andrews of the American Museum of Natural History, which [confirmed] that dinosaurs did, indeed, lay eggs.

"The *Protoceratops* exhibition is one part of our 'Walk in the Footsteps of the Dinosaurs' exhibit. Here [visitors will find] a one-tenth-scale habitat diorama of a dinosaur environment featuring five Jonas replicas,* the full, fossilized, mounted leg of a *Diplodocus*, an exhibit of modern animals that lived during the time of the dinosaurs, and three 'dinosaur digs' where children find replicas of bones and then identify them using a large key on the wall."

*A Jonas replica is a model or copy of a dinosaur created by the late Paul Jonas of New York. Although they are not up to current scientific thinking on how dinosaurs lived, they are admired as art as much as they are as science. Jonas models are displayed in such well-known museums as the Smithsonian Institution's National Museum of Natural History in Washington, D.C., and in smaller locations such as the dinosaur trackways in Glen Rose, Texas.

MINNESOTA

NIAGARA CAVE

Near the site of this natural cave is a gift shop and visitor center with a good fossil collection on display. Tours depart every half hour to give the visitor a closer look at this cave's amazing rock formations, including a sixty-foot "waterfall" formation.

Highway 139
Harmony, MN 55939
(507) 886-6606

Admission: Low fee

Facilities: Rest rooms, gift shop, wheelchair accessible

THE SCIENCE MUSEUM OF MINNESOTA

This museum's Paleontology Hall features a *Diplodocus* twenty feet high and eighty-two feet long, as well as an *Allosaurus* and a group of *Camptosaurus*. Special educational exhibits include a group of displays that illustrate what is and is not a true fossil in the geologic sense. Dinosaur eggs, a skull cast of *Tyrannosaurus rex*, and fossils of ancient crocodiles rare in Minnesota are also exhibited.

30 East Tenth Street
Saint Paul, MN 55101
(612) 221-9444, or
 (612) 221-9488

Admission: Low fee

Facilities: Rest rooms, gift shop, wheelchair accessible

Diplodocus

CURATOR'S CORNER

LYNNE KUJAWA

Public Relations
The Science Museum of Minnesota

Ms. Kujawa invites visitors to walk around and under the Science Museum of Minnesota's dinosaur group, which includes an eighty-two-foot-long *Diplodocus*, an *Allosaurus*, and two *Camptosaurus*: "The group was surrounded by glass walls for a period of time during 1991–1992 while they and the museum's paleontology hall were being renovated. The museum treated the reassembly process as an exhibit— 'Dinosaurs Going Up'—by keeping its dinosaurs and fossils available to visitors through special viewing windows. 'Bone phones' featured two-minute updates, and closed-circuit TV monitors were available for safe viewing of the arc-welding process.

"Since scientists reconstructed the last *Diplodocus* twenty-five years ago, paleontologists have discovered that this dinosaur's long tail curved up from the hips instead of angling down and dragging on the ground. *Diplodocus* mounts in all other museums are flat-footed, while the Science Museum of Minnesota's specimen stands on its toes, as research of its foot bones indicates it did millions of years ago."

MISSISSIPPI

MUSEUM OF NATURAL HISTORY, DELTA STATE UNIVERSITY

Most of the fossils on display here are from vertebrate and invertebrate animals that lived and thrived in an ancient sea that covered Mississippi during the time of the dinosaurs. But prehistoric mammals native to Mississippi are exhibited.

P.O. Box 3262
Cleveland, MS 38733
(601) 846-4496

Admission: Donation requested

Facilities: Rest rooms, food available, wheelchair accessible

---

CURATOR'S CORNER

ELEANOR DALY

Curator of Paleontology
Mississippi Museum of Natural Science

"Mississippi is not usually thought of as vertebrate fossil country," Ms. Daly says, "but the Magnolia State is quite rich in certain fossil specialties. Local fans hunt for bones of Ice Age mammals on river and creek bars in the western part of the state. Big mastodon and sloth remains are often found.

"In the Upper Eocene [35–40 million years ago] beds that cross the middle of the state, vertebrae and rib pieces of primitive whales can be had by fossil hunters, along with scarcer parts of sea snakes and sea cows. Sediments of the Age of Dinosaurs exist in the northeast corner of Mississippi, where the bones of mosasaur and large seagoing lizards have been collected, plus pieces of marine turtles and crocodiles.

"Though Mississippi is well endowed with vertebrate fossils, it is not dinosaur country. As you might have guessed, most of its sedimentary bedrock was laid down under a sea that spread north from the Gulf of Mexico at times in the past. Dinosaurs were never seagoing, so we seldom find their remains. Only a body or bone that has washed or floated offshore could have settled where we could dig it up now. That is why fossil collectors in Mississippi have so many shark teeth and so few dinosaurs."

MISSISSIPPI PETRIFIED FOREST

Arizona is not the only state where an ancient petrified forest can be found. Not only are many prehistoric trees preserved outdoors here, but a good cross-section of Mississippi's geological and paleontological history is exhibited in the site's museum and gift shop.

124 Forest Park Road
P.O. Box 37
Flora, MS 39071
(601) 879-8189

Admission: Low fee

Facilities: Rest rooms, gift shop, food available

MISSISSIPPI MUSEUM OF NATURAL SCIENCE

A fifteen-and-a-half-foot-long, 40-million-year-old whale-like creature—*Zygorhiza*—is suspended from the ceiling of this museum. *Zygorhiza* is, in fact, the Mississippi state fossil. Other prehistoric fossils are on display, including an ancient bison skull. But this is primarily a museum of more-modern wildlife and natural science.

111 North Jefferson
  Street
Jackson, MS 39202
(601) 354-7303

Admission: Low fee

Facilities: Rest rooms, gift shop, food available, wheelchair accessible

DUNN-SEILER MUSEUM

Mississippi may not be rich in dinosaur fossils, but this teaching museum has a reasonable fossil collection culled from the riches of other locales, including a *Triceratops* skull cast, a fossilized giant sea turtle shell, and a full skeletal cast of a saber-toothed cat. It also has an exhibit explaining how fossils are formed and preserved.

Mississippi State
  University
P.O. Drawer 5167
Mississippi State
  University, MS 39762
(601) 325-3915

Admission: Donation requested

Facilities: Rest rooms, gift shop, food available, wheelchair accessible

Zygorhiza

MISSOURI

MASTODON STATE PARK

Until a mammoth skeleton was excavated with a spearhead wedged in its side, there was no proof that man and the Ice Age beast coexisted. But scientists found just such a skeleton at Mastodon State Park in 1976. A replica is on display at the park visitors center. A marked path outside will help you retrace the steps that led paleontologists to the dig site so important in establishing a tie between man and mammoth. (See Curator's Corner.)

1551 Seckman Road
Imperial, MO 63052
(314) 464-2976

Admission: Low fee

Facilities: Rest rooms, gift shop, food available, wheelchair accessible

ST. LOUIS SCIENCE CENTER (AND DINOSAUR PARK)

The Dinosaur Park at this science center is more than a picnic area, as you might have guessed from the name. It is an area just outside the science center, "alive" with dinosaur reconstruction models including a *Triceratops* and a *Tyrannosaurus rex*. Inside, a new fossil center has a great many paleo resources, including more models, experimental videos about the changing theories of dinosaur lifestyles, and other related displays.

5050 Oakland Avenue
St. Louis, MO 63110
(314) 289-4444

Admission: Low fee

Facilities: Rest rooms, gift shop, food available, wheelchair accessible

Tyrannosaurus rex

CURATOR'S CORNER

DR. RUSS GRAHAM

Curator/Head of Geology
Illinois State Museum/Mastodon State Park

"Prehistorians and historians often feel like Sherlock Holmes, sleuthing through the foggy records of the past in order to reconstruct events and place them in perspective," Dr. Graham observes. "Prehistoric sites are like crime scenes without witnesses. These investigations depend upon physical evidence—biological remains—fossils, bones, teeth, plant parts, shells, and so on, buried in the earth.

"Historians and prehistorians are frequently drawn into their work by the sense of discovery. I have enjoyed the pursuit at the Kimmswick site or at 'bone beds' located about twenty miles south of St. Louis, at Mastodon State Park. Fossils of extinct Ice Age mammals, especially mastodons, have been found at this site since the early nineteenth century.

"A variety of private excavations occurred at the site until the early 1940s. One important event has been documented. Stone artifacts were found (circa 1907) with the bones of these extinct animals [suggesting that early man coexisted with these prehistoric giants]. The artifacts have been preserved at the Field Museum in Chicago. This was one of the first times this association was demonstrated in North America. But because the find was not scientifically documented, it was not generally accepted (and rightly so) by the scientific community.

"In 1979, I led excavations at Kimmswick. These excavations provided conclusive evidence that humans were associated with the extinct mastodons. Stone spearpoints and other stone artifacts were found with the bones of these and other animals. I am now researching the evidence. These studies should answer such questions as, 'What were the prehistoric people doing at Kimmswick?' and 'What was the relationship between the people and the prehistoric animals?'

"It has been fun for me to conduct inquiries into the past events of Kimmswick. I can't help but wonder how Sherlock Holmes might have approached this investigation."

MONTANA

MUSEUM OF THE ROCKIES

This is truly a world-class museum with a paleontological department headed by Dr. John R. Horner—the father of a *Maiasaura* nesting site affectionately called "Egg Mountain." Thanks in part to the watchful eyes of Rock Shop owner Marian Brandvold (see next entry), who found the first baby hadrosaur skeleton and showed it to the Montana dinosaur expert, a whole new species—*Maiasaura*, the "good mother lizard"—was discovered. Exhibits at the museum illustrate how duckbill dinosaurs might have cared for their young, and a great deal more.

Montana State
   University
600 West Kagy
   Boulevard
Bozeman, MT
   59717-0272
(406) 994-DINO, or
   (406) 994-2251

Admission: Low fee

Facilities: Rest rooms, gift shop, food available

CURATOR'S CORNER

DR. JOHN R. HORNER

Curator of Paleontology
Museum of the Rockies

"I was lucky enough to grow up in northern Montana where conditions are just right for preserving and exposing fossils," says Dr. Horner. "And since I was very small, I have been fascinated by the fossils I would find in the badlands around my home. I have always seen dinosaurs a little differently from the way most people do, and my research tends to reflect this difference. Instead of concentrating on finding new specimens and lots of them, I want to know how they lived and be able to convey a more complete idea about the living, breathing, functional animals that these bones represent.

"My studies have dealt mostly with *Maiasaura*. Because of several sites in Montana, we have 'snapshots' in time of how these animals lived. At the nesting grounds for these large animals, a range of sizes and developmental stages are preserved, which allows us to make inferences—educated guesses—about their growth rates, herding behaviors, and community interactions. Taking into account the environment in which they lived, we are also able to make estimations about the ecology of the total community of which these animals were a part."

PALEO FIELD SCHOOL

At this museum's field school, ordinary people of all ages can take on dinosaur dust with the pros in paleo field courses—some as short as a weekend, some much longer—in which university experts lead students on paleo exploration of Egg Mountain and other dig sites. Participants won't gain all the expertise of a trained paleontologist, but they will be surprised by how much they pick up, thanks to expert guidance and a wealth of fossil resources native to Montana.

Museum of the Rockies
Montana State
  University
Bozeman, MT 59717
(406) 994-2251

Admission: Not applicable, but there is a substantial fee for courses; write or phone for information.

Facilities: None

THE ROCK SHOP

If Marion Brandvold hadn't decided to stroll across the arid hills around this rock shop in search of fossils to display and sell (the same kind of fossils you will see or buy when you visit the shop), *Maiasaura* might never have been discovered. She saw tiny bones scattered across a hot, sandy hillside and had the presence of mind to gather them up. Once her son (now a paleontologist himself) saw and reconstructed the fossilized bits and pieces, the whole family knew this was something big—a baby dinosaur. The rest is paleontological history. Stop in and see (or buy) their latest discoveries.

P.O. Box 796
Bynum, MT 59419
(406) 469-2314

Admission: Free (but items are for sale)

Facilities: Rest rooms

PINE BUTTE SWAMP PRESERVE

This preserve is owned and overseen by the Nature Conservancy—a nonprofit group dedicated to preserving rare natural resources. The land was actually purchased to help protect the endangered plains grizzly bear, but the remarkable dig site here known as "Egg Mountain" enjoys that same protected status, thanks to the Nature Conservancy. Public tours are available, but you must write or call in advance.

HC 58, Box 34 B
Choteau, MT 59442
(406) 466-5526

Admission: Donation requested

Facilities: None

OLD TRAIL MUSEUM

This small local-history museum has a paleo perspective unique to towns rich in fossil finds. Alongside exhibits on local native people called Métis (pronounced *MAY-Tees*) are *Maiasaura* fossil remains. Future funding is expected to add hands-on exhibits for children to the small museum's educational offerings.

Teton Trail Village
Choteau, MT 59422
(406) 466-5332

Admission: Low fee

Facilities: Rest rooms, gift shop, wheelchair accessible

CARTER COUNTY MUSEUM

Big-time dinosaur finds are part of this small-town museum. A *Triceratops* skull, an *Anatosaurus* skeleton and a rare *Pachycephalosaurus* skull are on display, along with other exhibits of local interest.

100 Main Street
Ekalaka, MT 59324
(406) 775-6886

Admission: Low fee

Facilities: Rest rooms, gift shop, food nearby, wheelchair accessible

UPPER MUSSELSHELL VALLEY MUSEUM

A cast of *Avaceratops*—a small horned dinosaur collected from a nearby ranch in 1981–1982—is on display at this small local museum. The original skeleton is part of the University of Pennsylvania's paleo collection in Philadelphia. Also on display are various duckbill dinosaur fossils also collected at the *Avaceratops* dig site. Because Harlowtown is part of Montana's historic homestead area, the museum also features an 1800s-era schoolroom.

11 South Central Avenue
Harlowtown, MT 59036
(406) 632-5519

Admission: Donation requested

Facilities: Rest rooms, gift shop, wheelchair accessible

GARFIELD COUNTY MUSEUM

This museum, like the Carter County Museum (see above), houses some major dinosaur finds, thanks to the state's remarkable fossil resources. They have a good collection of *T. rex* bones along with a complete *Triceratops* and *Anatosaurus* (duckbill) skulls.

P.O. Box 325
Jordon, MT 59337
(406) 557-2224

Admission: Donation requested

Facilities: Rest rooms, gift shop, wheelchair accessible

CURATOR'S CORNER

JOHN AND MARION BRANDVOLD

The Rock Shop
Bynum, Montana

Marion Brandvold, owner of the Rock Shop in Bynum, Montana, has been a fossil hunter for most of her life. Early in 1978 she located a small mound of dirt that contained tiny, petrified bones. Marion collected the small pieces during the summer. Her son, David Trexler, began piecing the bones together and assembling a tiny skeleton. Dr. John R. Horner visited the Rock Shop in the fall of 1978, and was able to identify the specimens Marion had found as baby hadrosaurs. The rest is history.

NEBRASKA

TRAILSIDE MUSEUM

The mammoth is the state fossil of Nebraska, and a great specimen is on display at this University of Nebraska cooperative museum—a Colombian mammoth more than 30 million years old. Other prehistoric mammal fossils are also on display, and regular nature and geology tours are sponsored by the museum.

Fort Robinson State
 Park
Highway 20
Crawford, NE 69339
(308) 665-2929

Admission: Donation requested

Facilities: Rest rooms, gift shop, wheelchair accessible

WYO-BRASKA MUSEUM

Located on the Nebraska-Wyoming border, this small museum features a restoration model of one of the largest land mammals that ever roamed the earth—a *Baluchitherium* thirty feet long and nineteen feet tall. The original model, fabricated of plaster and asbestos, had to be destroyed, but artist Ron Kephart secured exclusive artist's rights to the enormous cast. Murals illustrate the fleshed-out beast and lifestyle differences between this mammal and *Triceratops*. Also on display in the museum's fossil room are the bones of mastodons, ancient turtles, and other Ice Age fossils. A small railroad museum is also on hand. A call ahead will assure you catered box lunches in a refurbished, air-conditioned dining car!

950 "U" Street
Gering, NE 69341
(308) 436-7104

Admission: Low fee

Facilities: Rest rooms, gift shop, food available (with advance notice), wheelchair accessible

AGATE FOSSIL BEDS NATIONAL MONUMENT

Nineteen million years ago, hundreds of animals met with a mysterious end and formed the Agate Fossil Beds, now considered one of the richest mammalian fossil bone beds in the United States. Among these are *Menoceras* (a two-horned, rhino-like animal), and *Moropus* (a strange mix of horse and rhino). The visitor center here offers a closer look at fossils from the bone bed as well as facts on the monument's history. Because the bone beds are still quite active—meaning a great many fossils have not yet been excavated—it is not uncommon to see paleontologists working when you visit.

P.O. Box 27
Gering, NE 69341
(308) 668-2211

Admission: Low fee

Facilities: Rest rooms, gift shop, wheelchair accessible

STATE MUSEUM OF NATURAL HISTORY

This museum is one of the top five paleontological museums in the United States. Known to many as "Elephant Hall," the museum has one of the most extensive collections of prehistoric elephant fossils. *Archidiskodon*—the world's largest mounted prehistoric elephant—is included, along with other prehistoric mammals. And although dinosaurs were not a part of Nebraska's prehistory, *Allosaurus* and *Stegosaurus* skeletal mounts are also on display. Don't miss the gift shop, "Dinosaurs Etc.," while you are there.

University of Nebraska
Morris Hall
14th and "U" Streets
Lincoln, NE 68588
(402) 472-2642, or
 (402) 472-0090
 (gift shop)

Admission: Donation requested

Facilities: Rest rooms, gift shop, food available, wheelchair accessible

ASHFALL FOSSIL BEDS STATE HISTORICAL PARK

Untold numbers of prehistoric mammals gathered at this state park, once an ancient watering hole. A sudden volcanic eruption emitted ash so thick that the animals were covered before they could escape, sealing their fate—freezing their fossilized bones and story in time for paleo experts and fans to explore today. You can follow the marked interpretive trail outside, and watch active teams excavate the bone bed in the "Rhino Barn"—a visitor center and working paleontology lab.

P.O. Box 66
Royal, NE 68773
(402) 893-2000

Admission: Low fee

Facilities: Rest rooms, gift shop, wheelchair accessible

CURATOR'S CORNER

DR. MICHAEL R. VOORHIES

Curator of Vertebrate Paleontology
University of Nebraska State Museum

Says Dr. Voorhies, "I grew up in a small town in northeastern Nebraska and became fascinated by the fossilized mammal teeth I found on the sandbars of the cool, clear streams near home. Some people grow out of their early love for fossils, but I never did. I studied geology at the University of Nebraska and worked for the State Museum in the summer, helping add to its enormous collection of fossil elephants, camels, rhinos and oreodonts. Later I was lucky enough to work with Morris Skinner, the greatest bone-hunter who ever prowled the canyons of northeastern Nebraska.

"The most exciting fossil deposit I've ever investigated is the volcanic ash bed at Ashfall Fossil Beds. It's like a prehistoric moment frozen in time."

NEVADA

BERLIN ICHTHYOSAUR STATE PARK

How did the fossil of a fifty-foot-long, seagoing reptile wind up at this state park in the Nevada desert? Simple! The land we call Nevada was once under a huge, prehistoric ocean. The park has a Fossil Shelter that features nine fossilized sea serpents. Remember—these may have been "fish lizards" (that's what ichthyosaur actually means), but they had no gills; they surfaced like modern whales to breathe. And evidence from a German ichthyosaur fossil site suggests that the *ichthyosaurs*, instead of laying eggs like most marine reptiles, bore their young live.

HC 61, Box 61200
Austin, NV 89310-9301
(702) 964-9301

Admission: Low fee

Facilities: Rest rooms, gift shop, wheelchair accessible

LAS VEGAS NATURAL HISTORY MUSEUM

Once located on the opposite end of town, the relocated museum has been down-sized considerably. However, a good selection of dinosaur skeletons is still on display along with interpretive exhibits on prehistory.

900 Las Vegas
  Boulevard North
Las Vegas, NV 89101
(702) 384-3466

Admission: Low fee

Facilities: Rest rooms, gift shop, food available, wheelchair accessible

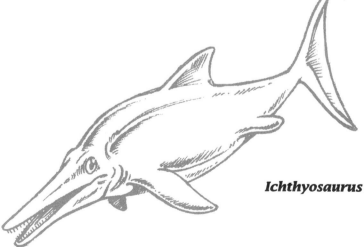

Ichthyosaurus

CURATOR'S CORNER

DANIEL DURALL

Exhibits and Collections Coordinator
Las Vegas Natural History Museum

"The Las Vegas Natural History Museum's prehistoric room has an extensive dinosaur collection," Mr. Durall says. "The central exhibit is a half-scale animated *T. rex* and a three-quarters-scale animated *Triceratops*. An animated *Ankylosaurus* with nest and animated hatchlings has just been completed.

"Static exhibits include life-size re-creations of *Archaeopteryx* and *Compsognathus* attacking a dragonfly. The exhibit demonstrates the anatomical similarities between these two animals. Other re-creations include three full-sized *Sauronithoides* attacking a primitive mammal that has broken into a *Parasaurolophus* nest. The mother *Parasaurolophus* is running back to protect her nest."

NEW HAMPSHIRE

LITTLE NATURE MUSEUM

 Sandra Martin, the owner of this private museum, is a teacher, devoted to teaching natural science to children and adults—even fellow teachers on the East Coast. And she shares her lifelong passion for fossils by displaying thousands of fossil specimens at her museum, which happens to be her home as well. Seashells, rocks, and bird mounts are also on display. A call in advance is necessary to explore her amazing collection.

59 Boyce Road
Weare, NH 03281
(603) 529-7180

Admission: Free

Facilities: Rest rooms

CURATOR'S CORNER

SANDRA W. MARTIN

Curator/Owner
Little Nature Museum

Ms. Martin calls the Little Nature Museum "quite unconventional: It is in my home, is a private collection, and is open by appointment only. I opened my museum [almost forty] years ago, as a childhood hobby. Since that time, I have had an interest in fossils. My collection of fossils has grown over the years, thanks to gifts from interested friends. Fossils are rarely ever found in New Hampshire, and those that have been found are of poor quality.

"My collection is composed primarily of small invertebrate and plant fossils and some vertebrates—including dinosaurs. I have cataloged 444 individual specimens in my public display collection.

These are all on open shelves, where visitors are encouraged to handle them. There are probably fifty or so more specimens not on display, which are yet to be cataloged and/or identified.

"The unfortunate thing about eighty-five percent of the collection is that other than identification of the specimens, little or no information is available. Almost all information that should have accompanied the specimens was either never recorded or has been lost over time. I am sure that many specimens were collected in the early 1900s. The fossils are from all parts of the United States."

NEW JERSEY

MORRIS MUSEUM

Funded by a combination of local, state, corporate and private sources, this museum has dinosaur tracks on exhibit, as well as a *Stegosaurus* reconstruction model and a similar reconstruction of the flying reptile *Pteranodon*.

6 Normandy Heights
  Road
Morristown, NJ 07960
(201) 538-0454

Admission: Donation requested

Facilities: Rest rooms, gift shop, wheelchair accessible

RUTGERS GEOLOGY MUSEUM

Dinosaur tracks, found in great numbers in the state of New Jersey, are on display here, along with a mastodon skeleton rescued from a circus. All bones—apart from the tusks and leg bones—are actual fossilized originals.

College Avenue
New Brunswick, NJ
  08903
(908) 932-7243

Admission: Donation requested

Facilities: Rest rooms, gift shop, wheelchair accessible

CURATOR'S CORNER

DR. DAVID PARRIS

Curator
New Jersey State Museum

"Although America's first dinosaur finds came out of New Jersey, many people are unaware of the importance of current New Jersey dinosaur discoveries," says Dr. Parris. "The New Jersey State Museum's Ellisdale Site, discovered by Bob Denton and Bob O'Neil, and the Inversand Site, owned by the Hungerford family, are especially exciting places for searching out Cretaceous dinosaurs and other fossil creatures.

"Many are on display at the museum in Trenton. The museum's discovery of fossil mammals at the Ellisdale Dinosaur Site has given added importance to its collection. These fossil teeth are virtually all that is known of Cretaceous mammals in eastern North America."

BERGEN MUSEUM OF ART AND SCIENCE

New Jersey mastodon bones are central to this smaller museum's fossil collection. Also featured are a children's discovery room and several other science and art exhibits.

Ridgewood and
  Fairview avenues
Paramus, NJ 07652
(201) 265-1248

Admission: Low fee

Facilities: Rest rooms, gift shop, wheelchair accessible

JENKINSON'S AQUARIUM

Featured at this traditional aquarium is a unique fossil room dedicated to the exploration of ancient marine life and the comparison of old with new. In addition to the exotic fish is a hands-on "touch tank," as well as a few tropical birds and mammals.

Boardwalk and
  Parkway
Point Pleasant Beach,
  NJ 08742
(908) 899-1659

Admission: Low fee

Facilities: Rest rooms, gift shop, food available, wheelchair accessible

PRINCETON NATURAL HISTORY MUSEUM

A baby *Maiasaura* replica—modeled after those found by Montana paleontologist Jack Horner, is one of this university museum's outstanding exhibits, although skeletal mounts of an *Allosaurus* and Ice Age mammals (including an Irish elk) are also on display. Call in advance for changing hours and exhibits.

Guyot Halls
Washington Street
Princeton University
Princeton, NJ 08544
(609) 258-1322

Admission: Donation requested

Facilities: Rest rooms, gift shop, food available, wheelchair accessible

NEW JERSEY STATE MUSEUM

The well-known paleontologist Dr. David Parris is the curator of this fine state museum's paleo resources, which include hadrosaur or duckbill dinosaur fossil evidence, which is so much a part of the Garden State's prehistoric record. In fact, one of the United States' first dinosaur species was found in New Jersey. Ice Age mammal fossils are also on exhibit. Call ahead for information on special children's dinosaur programming, such as the "Dino Safari" offered in the past.

205 West State Street
Trenton, NJ 08625-0530
(609) 292-6308

Admission: Low fee

Facilities: Rest rooms, gift shop, wheelchair accessible

THE DINO-TREKKING SITES 83

NEW MEXICO

RUTH HALL MUSEUM OF PALEONTOLOGY

 This museum displays the more than 100 complete skeletons of *Coelophysis*, one of the smallest carnivorous dinosaurs (but bloodthirsty nonetheless), that have been found at Ghost Ranch. Fossil evidence suggests that when food was scarce, adult *Coelophysis* may well have eaten their young some 225 million years ago. The museum is at the site of a Presbyterian Church–owned conference center, so, although visitors are welcome, they should be respectful of the religious and other conference groups often in attendance at Ghost Ranch.

Ghost Ranch
  Conference Center
Abiquiu, NM 87501
(505) 685-4333

Admission: Low fee

Facilities: Rest rooms, gift shop, food available, wheelchair accessible

NEW MEXICO MUSEUM OF NATURAL HISTORY

 Featured on dinosaur television programs, this museum has a wealth of paleontological wonders to offer, including the "Evolator," an evolutionary elevator through 70 million years of time. Lifelike scenes include a *Parasaurolophus* mother and her young. Other dinosaurs featured at this museum are *Stegosaurus*, *Camarasaurus*, and *Coelophysis*, as well as the pterosaur *Quetzalcoatlus*. Outside are sculptures of *Pentaceratops* and *Albertosaurus* by the award-winning artist David A. Thomas.

1801 Mountain Road
  N.W.
Albuquerque, NM 87104
(505) 841-8837

Admission: Low fee

Facilities: Rest rooms, gift shop, food available, wheelchair accessible

UNIVERSITY OF NEW MEXICO GEOLOGY MUSEUM

 Prehistoric fossils, many native to New Mexico, are featured at this small teaching museum. Dinosaur tracks and *Coelophysis* skeletal casts are just two significant exhibits.

Albuquerque, NM
  87125
(505) 277-4204

Admission: Donation requested

Facilities: Rest rooms, food available, wheelchair accessible

CLAYTON LAKE STATE PARK

Unauthorized collecting of paleontological relics has become a lucrative enterprise and a huge problem in recent years. Large numbers of dinosaur tracks were found at this locale in 1982, but the site was declared a protected state park only after it became clear that tracks were being snatched up illegally. Thanks to careful management, those tracks, along with *Pterodactyl* handprints, can yet be seen in the New Mexico sandstone, (along with tracks of an unidentified web-footed dinosaur). You can find maps at the park's ranger station.

(fifteen miles northwest of Clayton)
N.M. Route 370
Clayton, NM 88415
(505) 374-8808

Admission: Low fee

Facilities: Rest rooms, gift shop, wheelchair accessible

MCKEE CARSON MUSEUM

This is primarily a museum of local history rather than paleontology. But because dinosaurs are so much a part of New Mexico's ancient past, some fossils and minerals are included in the exhibits.

309 West Main Street
Farmington, NM 87401
(505) 327-1347

Admission: Donation requested

Facilities: Rest rooms, gift shop, wheelchair accessible

FOLSOM MUSEUM

One of the original New Mexico "natives"—the Folsom Man—is on exhibit at this museum. This is clearly not an exhibit on dinosaurs, but it's worth a brief stop for its pre-historical value.

Main Street
Folsom, NM 88419
(505) 278-2155

Admission: Donation requested

Facilities: Rest rooms, gift shop, wheelchair accessible

BLACKWATER DRAW MUSEUM

There is a special exhibit devoted to New Mexico's Ice Age mammals at this small museum, and some other fossils are also on display.

U.S. Route 70
Portales, NM 88130
(505) 562-2254

Admission: Low fee

Facilities: Rest rooms, wheelchair accessible

MINERALOGICAL MUSEUM

 Fossils from New Mexico and other places are on display at this teaching museum. The size and variety of the collection—more than 9,000 specimens—make this museum worth the stop.

New Mexico Institute
  of Mining and
  Technology
Socorro, NM 87801
(505) 835-5420

Admission: Donation requested

Facilities: Rest rooms, gift shop, wheelchair accessible

CURATOR'S CORNER

DR. SPENCER G. LUCAS, PH.D.

Curator of Paleontology
New Mexico Museum of Natural History and Science

Dr. Lucas made scientific headlines in the spring of 1994 (along with a great many other paleontologists in a cooperative research team) by uncovering dinosaur footprints that did, indeed, predate the earliest known dinosaur prints found in the American southwest. Speaking of the work of the New Mexico Museum of Natural History and Science, he says, "A vigorous research program has focused, since 1988, on the Late Triassic period, the time of dinosaur origins. Fieldwork throughout New Mexico and the adjoining states has uncovered more than half a dozen new Triassic dinosaurs and many other new fossil fishes, amphibians, and non-dinosaurian reptiles, as well as the oldest mammal known.

"Our research shows that dinosaurs appeared suddenly over a wide area—Argentina, Brazil, Morocco, India, the United States—about 225 million years ago. At their first appearance, dinosaurs were diverse and specialized. This suggests that the actual origin of the dinosaurs may long predate their earliest fossils.

"Where and how did the dinosaur originate? We really don't know."

NEW YORK

NEW YORK STATE MUSEUM
NEW YORK STATE GEOLOGICAL SURVEY

 This state-run museum has somewhat shifted its focus away from earth sciences, including paleontology. But several good exhibits are still in place, including a diorama of a mastodon mother and her calf, and a group of dinosaur tracks. Other bits and pieces are also on display. (See Curator's Corner.)

State Education Center
Albany, NY 12230
(518) 474-5877

Admission: Donation requested

Facilities: Rest rooms, gift shop, wheelchair accessible

CURATOR'S CORNER

DR. BRYN J. MADER

Collections Registrar, Department of Mammalogy
American Museum of Natural History

"As long as I can remember," says Dr. Mader, "I have loved extinct animals, especially dinosaurs. My parents brought me to the American Museum often as a child. In fact, I often begged them to take me. They always encouraged my interest. From high school on, I knew I wanted to be a professional paleontologist, and spent my college and graduate years training for this career.

"In recent years I have been privileged to work in the museum that I loved so much as a child—the American Museum of Natural History. I spend my days caring for the massive collections of fossils kept mostly 'behind the scenes,' and thus rarely seen by the public.

"Initially I worked for the Department of Vertebrate Paleontology, but I am now Collections Registrar for the Department of Vertebrate Mammalogy. It is an honor to care for these collections—and a great responsibility. The collections of the American Museum have taken well over a century to build, and are irreplaceable. It is my job to ensure that they are preserved for posterity, so that future generations will always have them to learn from and enjoy.

"My research includes the dinosaurs and *Titanotheres*—an extinct relative of the horse and rhino, with large, forked horns. Paleontology is a fascinating subject, and I can't think of a more rewarding career for a young person to enter."

BUFFALO MUSEUM OF SCIENCE

"Dinosaurs and Company" is the name of the exhibit you'll want to see first at this museum. Skeletal mounts of a juvenile *Allosaurus* and *Triceratops* are joined by dinosaur eggs, teeth, and skin impressions. Other prehistoric animals featured include marine reptiles such as mosasaurs, as well as pterosaurs and prehistoric mammals, including the oldest known bat.

1020 Humbolt
  Parkway
Buffalo, NY
  14211-1293
(716) 896-5200

Admission: Low fee

Facilities: Rest rooms, gift shop, wheelchair accessible

DURHAM CENTER MUSEUM

Fossils of plant life dating back 250 to 300 million years are a large part of this once-private collection, now gone public. Although Vernon Haskin, the collections original owner, only finished the 8th grade, he went on to become one of New York State's foremost fossil experts, leading scientists and students on fossil tours of the area. Museum curator Vernona Fleurent (Haskin's daughter) will be happy to guide you through the fossil collection and her father's career.

Route 145
East Durham, NY 12423
(518) 239-4313

Admission: Donation requested

Facilities: Rest rooms, gift shop

AMERICAN MUSEUM OF NATURAL HISTORY

One of the most amazing museums in the United States—in fact, one of the best in the world—the American Museum has inspired many a visitor to work in the paleontological field. Not just one, but *three* dinosaur halls, featuring an extensive collection of mounted dinosaur skeletons, are waiting for you to explore. *Tyrannosaurus rex*, *Stegosaurus*, *Apatosaurus*, *Barosaurus*, and *Allosaurus* are only a few. But don't miss the extensive collection of prehistoric mammals including the gigantic "bear-dog" *Amphicyon* and the educational exhibit on early hominids (ancestors of modern man) while you are there.

79th Street and Central
  Park West
New York, NY
  10024-5192
(212) 769-5100

Admission: Low fee

Facilities: Rest rooms, gift shop, food available, wheelchair accessible

CURATOR'S CORNER

DR. ED LANDING

New York State Paleontologist/Curator
New York State Museum

Men and women of science have been studying the rich fossil record of New York since the 1840s, when the theory of relative time correlation was first being mapped out and tested. By comparing New York fossils in certain rocks with those in countries in Europe and Asia, scientists were able to set a standard for just what combination of rock and fossilized life-forms existed in each time frame. Like the sure knowledge that blue and yellow will combine to make green, science determined that the fossil/rock combinations would prove just as reliable in determining geological time. "In a sense," says Dr. Landing,

"New York State is the standard for all North American Paleozoic time correlations."

Another unique facet of working in New York, according to Dr. Landing, is the great variety of early specimens available within the distance of a relatively short drive. "There are two separate continents," Dr. Landing says of the area once divided by an ancient sea. In New York State, the fossils indicate that animals thrived in warm waters, but only a couple of hundred miles away, around Boston, the fossil record says cold water sustained an entirely different kind of life.

NATURAL STONE BRIDGE AND CAVES

The only prehistoric fossils found at this location are in the Caveman Rock Shop. Though the collection for sale is quite impressive, don't underestimate the prehistoric appeal of the caves and natural bridges. You can take a guided tour of the caves, and there are interpretive trails explaining the bridges. Geologists estimate the age of the rocky wonders age at between 1.1 and 1.2 billion years.

HC 1, Box 22
Stone Bridge Road
Pottersville, NY 12860
(518) 494-2283

Admission: Moderate fee

Facilities: Rest rooms, gift shop, food available, wheelchair accessible

LAKE CHAMPLAIN

 Scotland's Loch Ness Monster has a rival in the United States, thanks to the legend of "Champ." More than fifty people are so sure of their sea-monster sightings that they've had their names carved into a roadside sign. Whether or not you believe in a prehistoric survivor, the area's "Champ Day" celebration is great fun for dinosaur fans (the first Saturday in August, in years past—but call the Chamber of Commerce to be certain). And Vermont investigator Richard Duelle just might change your mind during his annual report of Champ evidence. You take your chances as far as sightings go, but nearly every business in the area offers great Champ memorabilia and favorite stories.

c/o Moriah Chamber
of Commerce
Port Henry, New York
12974
(518) 546-7261 or
(518) 546-3341
(town clerk's office)

Admission: Free

Facilities: Rest rooms, wheelchair accessible

Plesiosaur

NORTH CAROLINA

AURORA FOSSIL MUSEUM

This museum's multimedia tour covers fossils native to North Carolina, most from local phosphate mines. Marine animals (early whales and sharks, among others) and the Ice Age mastodon are represented by teeth and bone fragments as well as a huge prehistoric whale skull and a shark jawbone. But the unique and perhaps the best thing about this tour comes at the end, when visitors are offered the chance to sift through phosphate mine tailings (leftovers) for common but real fossils. What you find, you can keep.

P.O. Box 352
Aurora, NC 27806
(919) 322-4238

Admission: Low fee

Facilities: Rest rooms, gift shop, wheelchair accessible

NORTH CAROLINA MARITIME MUSEUM

Prehistoric fossils are a surprising part of this museum, which is devoted mainly to shipping. During the summer months, special fossil-study programs for kids are offered. And an annual Fossil Festival takes place in the fall. Call in advance for specific dates and details.

315 Front Street
Beaufort, NC 28516
(919) 728-7317

Admission: Donation requested

Facilities: Rest rooms, gift shop, wheelchair accessible

DISCOVERY PLACE

A prehistoric exhibit featuring a fossil collection of moderate size is this museum's "regular" offering. But the animated dinosaurs from Dinamation International visit on a regular basis (on average, about every eighteen months). Call ahead for details, or stop by and see for yourself.

301 North Tryon Street
Charlotte, NC 28202
(704) 372-6261, or
 (800) 935-0553

Admission: Moderate fee

Facilities: Rest rooms

NORTH CAROLINA MUSEUM OF LIFE AND SCIENCE

 Stroll down the "Prehistory Trail" at this museum for a look at our planet's dinosaur history. The outdoor models are classics, older and slightly the worse for wear, but well worth a closer look. Inside, the geology department offers some fossils native to the area, and a cast of a *Tyrannosaurus rex* skull. Also, several "hands-on" exhibits for kids.

433 Murray Avenue
Durham, NC 27705
(919) 220-5429

Admission: Low fee

Facilities: Rest rooms, gift shop, wheelchair accessible

RANKIN MUSEUM OF AMERICAN HERITAGE

 This museum offers more regional recorded history than prehistoric finds, but a good cross-section of fossils is on display.

302 West Church
Ellerbe, NC 28338
(919) 652-6378

Admission: Donation requested

Facilities: Rest rooms, gift shop, wheelchair accessible

SCHIELE MUSEUM OF NATURAL HISTORY

 This museum's "Hall of Earth and Man" is a visual walk through time, following the geological record and the progression of life on Earth. With both dioramas and fossil samples ranging from the earliest life-forms to early reptiles to dinosaurs (scale models) to the evolution of man, the exhibits track the most significant changes, as well as illustrating how fossils are formed and how scientists collect the fossils they find.

1500 East Garrison
  Boulevard
Gastonia, NC 28054
(704) 866-6900

Admission: Donation requested

Facilities: Rest rooms, gift shop, wheelchair accessible

NATURAL SCIENCE CENTER

 State tourism literature doesn't begin to do this learning center justice. In addition to a "Dinosaur Gallery" featuring a *Tyrannosaurus rex* restoration model and a *Triceratops* skeletal mount, as well as a room full of fossil exhibits, the Natural Science Center has a petting zoo, a planetarium, and dozens of other fine elements for families to explore.

4301 Lawndale Drive
Greensboro, NC 27401
(919) 288-3769

Admission: Moderate fee

Facilities: Rest rooms, gift shop, food available, wheelchair accessible

CURATOR'S CORNER

DR. KENNETH A. BRIDLE

Director of Exhibits
SciWorks

"SciWorks, the Science Center and Environmental Park of Forsyth County, has been in existence as a nature and children's museum for about twenty years," says Dr. Bridle. "Recently we have received funding and support for major renovations and expansion to increase our exhibit area, add a planetarium, and improve the utilization of, and access to, our thirty-acre facility.

"In July of 1993 we opened a special exhibit of robotic dinosaurs, which ran through October. In conjunction with this exhibit, we have developed an exhibit of fossils concentrating on those from our area. We have only a small number of fossils and some casts in our permanent collection. However, we have borrowed a large amount of material from other North Carolina and Virginia museums.

"We were mainly interested in dinosaur fossils, to help illustrate the history of life on Earth. While searching for this material, though, we found that North Carolina is rich in fossil deposits, both marine and terrestrial. We found that the state has several rock layers that have been sites of discovery for many kinds of dinosaurs, insects, and the more recent large mammals. We have made connections with local geologists and paleontologists to help us provide curators' tours of a local site that has several kinds of fossil and dinosaur footprints. We also have arranged a lecture series that will provide teacher in-service credit in geology."

NORTH CAROLINA MUSEUM OF NATURAL SCIENCE

Skull replicas seem to be a favorite at this state museum. Represented are *Tyrannosaurus rex*, *Triceratops*, and the Ice Age saber-toothed cat. The bird hall includes a full cast of the famed German *Archaeopteryx* discovery. Don't miss the whale skeleton suspended from the ceiling of the hall of mammals.

102 North Salisbury Street
Raleigh, NC 27604
(910) 733-7450

Admission: Low fee

Facilities: Rest rooms, gift shop, wheelchair accessible

THE DINO-TREKKING SITES 93

SCIWORKS

This hands-on museum is a work in progress, as far as dinosaurs go. More fossils and models are being added as funding allows. And traveling dinosaur exhibits are a regular part of this museum's exciting schedule. SciWorks is committed to making entertaining, educational exhibits available to visitors, and it shows.

400 Hanes Mill Road
Winston-Salem, NC
 27105
(910) 767-6730

Admission: Low fee

Facilities: Rest rooms, gift shop, food available

Archaeopteryx

NORTH DAKOTA

DAKOTA DINOSAUR MUSEUM

June 1994 marked the grand opening of this 13,500-square-foot dinosaur museum, complete with ten full-scale dinosaur skeletons and a life-size model of *Triceratops*. In addition to a library containing dinosaur material, the museum has a children's corner and a working fossil lab. Be sure to call ahead for information on specially scheduled paleo classes in the field.

1226 Simms
Dickinson, ND 58601
(701) 227-0431

Admission: Low fee

Facilities: Rest rooms, gift shop, wheelchair accessible

JOACHIM REGIONAL MUSEUM

This museum is the temporary home of the Dakota Dinosaur Museum's collection prior to its 1994 opening. A few fossils from *Triceratops* and *Tyrannosaurus rex* are scheduled to remain on site, but call ahead for the most accurate information. Be sure to ask about children's paleontology camps in nearby Marmarth.

Visitor's Center
314 Third Avenue West
Dickinson, ND 58601
(701) 225-4988

Admission: Donation requested

Facilities: Rest rooms, wheelchair accessible

LEONARD HALL MUSEUM

Dinosaur murals on the building's outer walls and an authentic *Triceratops* skull inside are the only paleo resources on display at this geology museum, but it's an interesting place to stretch your legs while in North Dakota.

University of North Dakota
P.O. Box 8068
University Station
Grand Forks, ND 58202
(701) 777-2011

Admission: Donation requested

Facilities: Rest rooms, gift shop, food available, wheelchair accessible

CURATOR'S CORNER

LARRY LEAGUE

Dakota Dinosaur Museum

"Hiking the badlands of southwestern North Dakota early in the morning as the sun peeks over the rugged buttes—what an exhilarating experience!" Professor League exults. "Yet it begins a typical day in the life of a dinosaur hunter."

"The thrill of not knowing what exciting fossil is exposed just around the next hill keeps you searching for more bones, even as the hot noonday sun intensifies and sweat runs down your brow. To suddenly look down and see a complete *Tyrannosaurus rex* tooth staring you in the eye? Well, folks, it's Christmas in June for the dinosaur hunter.

"With our new Dakota Dinosaur Museum facilities, we hope to provide similar experiences for the general public by offering summer dinosaur digs. Believe me, it's an experience you will treasure for a lifetime."

OHIO

MCKINLEY MUSEUM OF HISTORY

 "Discovery World" at the McKinley Museum has a fine collection of dinosaur exhibits, including a fully animated robotic model of an *Allosaurus* that seems to have a mind of its own when it comes to working. But, moving or not, it's a great model. Also on display is a dig-site reproduction, complete with partially exposed replicas of dinosaur bones, and more. Don't miss seeing NASA's "Space Station Earth" while you are there.

800 McKinley
  Monument Drive NW
Canton, OH 44708-4800
(216) 455-7043

Admission: Low fee

Facilities: Rest rooms, gift shop, food available, wheelchair accessible

CURATOR'S CORNER

BETH KRANTZ

Director
Discovery World/McKinley Museum

Ms. Krantz speaks proudly of the McKinley Museum's unique, interactive science facility: "Discovery World, designed by Edwin Schlossberg, Inc., is divided into three islands: Natural History, Ecology, and Space. The Natural History island is dedicated to telling the story of the past.

"It begins with local history at the Paleo-Indian hut. This represents a Clovis campsite that was discovered at Nobles Pond in Jackson Township, Stark County, Ohio. McKinley Museum is the curator of the artifacts found at this site. Children enjoy sifting for artifacts in the simulated archaeological dig (near the Paleo-Indian hut) Our own mastodon, 'Bondo Betty,' found not far from the museum, towers in the foreground of the Paleo campsite.

"At the entrance of Discovery World, our robot *Allosaurus* greets visitors. 'Alice' was created in London by artist Robby Braun. Her fabrication was covered in the Walter Cronkite 'Dinosaur!' series. We also have reproductions of the *Triceratops* and *Tyrannosaurus rex* skulls from the American Museum of Natural History in New York. The *T. rex* skull is nestled in a cave that allows children to climb up and stick their heads in the jaws. Adults also love the photo opportunity.

"Interactive laser-disc programs invite visitors to explore archaeology and dinosaurs in depth. Discovery World is not a natural-history museum, but a science center that challenges visitors to explore, question, and delve deeper into the fascinating world of science."

CINCINNATI MUSEUM OF NATURAL HISTORY

 An outstanding display of Ice Age mammals is on display here, in a relatively new Pleistocene habitat exhibit. Visitors can walk through the landscape to get a close-up look at ancient animal reconstructions, including a seven-foot ancient bison, a huge ground sloth, and a giant beaver. Many consider this one of the best Ice Age mammal exhibits ever created.

1301 Western Avenue
Cincinnati, OH 45203
(513) 287-7000

Admission: Low fee

Facilities: Rest rooms, gift shop, wheelchair accessible

THE CLEVELAND MUSEUM OF NATURAL HISTORY

 A wealth of prehistoric discoveries awaits you at this museum. Specimens on display include *Dunkleosteus* (an ancient armored fish), *Nanotyrannus* (sometimes called a smaller cousin to *Tyrannosaurus rex*), and a seventy-foot-long sauropod recently identified as *Haplocanthosaurus*. Also worth seeing is the Ice Age mammal exhibit and a replica of "Lucy," one of the oldest hominids ever found.

1 Wade Oval Drive
University Circle
Cleveland, OH
  44106-1767
(216) 231-4600

Admission: Low fee

Facilities: Rest rooms, gift shop, wheelchair accessible

OHIO HISTORICAL CENTER

 Here you'll find more proof of the prevalence of mastodons in Ohio's prehistoric past. The mastodon skeleton on display here was discovered on a farm in 1894. A small collection of other fossils native to Ohio is also on display.

Interstate 71 and
  17th Avenue
Columbus, OH 43211
(614) 297-2350

Admission: Donation requested

Facilities: Rest rooms, gift shop, wheelchair accessible

DAYTON MUSEUM OF NATURAL HISTORY

 Southwest Ohio is famous for its rich trilobite discoveries—the largest of which is on display at the Smithsonian's National Museum of Natural History in Washington, D.C. A small temporary exhibit at the Dayton Museum will be replaced with a more ambitious effort in 1995, centered around the "butterflies of the sea"—the ancient trilobites.

DeWeese Parkway
Dayton, OH 45414
(513) 275-7431

Admission: Low fee

Facilities: Rest rooms, gift shop, wheelchair accessible

CAESAR CREEK LAKE

Visitors can obtain a free permit from the U.S. Army Corp of Engineers at the address listed, along with directions to the lake spillway. With that permit, you are allowed to keep as much marine invertebrate material as you can carry in the palms of your hands. Trilobites, shark's teeth, and brachiopods are just a few of the fossils commonly found at the spillway. But don't forget the permit! No permit, no take-home fossil finds.

Caesar Creek Lake Corp
 of Engineers
4848 North Clarksville
Waynesville, OH 45068
(513) 897-1050, or
 (513) 897-3055
 (visitor center)

Admission: Free

Facilities: Rest rooms, gift shop, wheelchair accessible

CURATOR'S CORNER

MS. JUDY CHOVAN

Curator
Dayton Museum of Natural History

"Six hundred million years ago, trilobites swam over, walked on, and burrowed into the sediments of the ocean floor," says Ms. Chovan. "Like crabs, lobsters, and shrimp of today, they were scavengers and predators. Trilobites had hard external protective skeletons, similar to medieval knights' suits of armor. Joints in the skeleton allowed trilobites to roll up into a ball for defense, just like the pillbugs you can see in your backyard today.

"As a trilobite grew, it had to shed or molt its hard exoskeleton to grow a larger one with more room inside. So each trilobite left behind many shells— that's one reason we find so many fossil trilobites. Shrimp and crabs grow the same way today.

"Around eighty million years ago, the area around Dayton was underwater— covered by a shallow sea. Trilobites were everywhere. Around 250 million years ago, they all disappeared. No one knows why they went extinct. But they were around far longer than people have been, so far."

OKLAHOMA

OKLAHOMA MUSEUM OF NATURAL HISTORY

An outstanding exhibit on prehistoric mammals is at the top of this museum's paleo resources. A rare horned rodent, *Epigaulus hatcheri*, is on display, along with better-known ancient mammals such as ground sloths, giant bison, and early camels. The highlight of the museum's dinosaur collection is bones from a baby *Apatosaurus*.

1335 Asp Avenue
Norman, OK 73019
(405) 325-4712

Admission: Donation requested

Facilities: Rest rooms, gift shop, wheelchair accessible

DINOSAUR TRACK SITE

Generations of visitors have explored these trackways in southern Oklahoma. As a schoolgirl more than fifty years ago, Thelma Lea Ketchum, the author's grandmother, saw the tracks during a school field trip. According to Mrs. Ketchum, even then, seeing the enormous footprints gave kids a rare glimpse into ancient natural history. Because the tracks are a favorite part of the town's distinctive history, a two-story metal sculpture of a sauropod was commissioned to stand outside the local museum of history, where Norma Gene Young, the town historian, will gladly tell you about the prehistoric finds of the region.

Cimarron Heritage
  Center
P.O. Box 1146
Boise City, OK 73933
(405) 544-3479

Admission: Free

Facilities: Rest rooms, gift shop

DINOSAUR QUARRIES

These dinosaur tracks, along with a monument to what are called *Brontosaurus* (*Apatosaurus*) bones on site, are a private collection on private property. Although the owners try to accommodate visitors, don't expect a tour without phoning in advance. Postmistress Bonnie Heppard is the local contact.

c/o Bonnie Heppard
P.O. Box 36
Kenton, OK 73946
(405) 261-7474

Admission: No fee

Facilities: None

CURATOR'S CORNER

NORMA JEAN YOUNG

Town Historian
Boise City, Oklahoma

"I was six years old when dinosaur fossils were uncovered eight miles east of Kenton (thirty miles northwest of Boise City) in 1931," Ms. Young remembers. "The best find was the almost-complete skeleton of a seventy-foot *Apatosaurus.*

"Dinosaur tracks were also found embedded in rock in a streambed northeast of Kenton. This was even better, as far as the kids were concerned, because this was something that would stay here—we could see them anytime we wished. We now have bus tours to the Kenton area early in June, and the tourists (and locals) never tire of slipping and sliding down that arroyo to view the huge tracks. They realize, 'I am walking where a dinosaur once walked.'

"Some experts believed the dinosaur finds here were farther east than any other discoveries of the Jurassic period, and that if it were possible to use a giant scraper to take off that top layer of soil over most of Cimarron County, millions more dinosaur fossils would be exposed."

OREGON

HANCOCK FIELD STATION
JOHN DAY FOSSIL BEDS NATIONAL MONUMENT

The Oregon Museum of Science and Industry offers a series of field classes at this Clarno unit of the John Day Fossil Beds National Monument. This field station is not yet open to the general public, but plans are on the table, so write (in advance) for any possible updates and opportunities. These are ancient plant and mammal fossil resources, rather than dinosaurs.

Fossil, OR 97830

Admission: Free

Facilities: Rest rooms

PREHISTORIC GARDENS

Sculptor E. V. Nelson began his work with prehistoric creatures in 1953. As a result, his work obviously does not always match modern dinosaur theory, but with more than a dozen well maintained "creatures" scattered throughout an Oregon rain forest, the stop is well worth your time, "accurate" or not.

36848 Highway 101 South
Port Orford, OR 97465
(503) 332-4463

Admission: Low fee

Facilities: Rest rooms, gift shop, food available, wheelchair accessible

JOHN DAY FOSSIL BED NATIONAL MONUMENT

Life spanning 40 million years is well represented in the fossil record at this national monument. Once a subtropic home to early alligators, three-toed horses, and many other creatures, the thriving habitat was apparently buried by mud slides resulting from sudden volcanic activity. There are marked interpretive trails and a visitor center. Scientists at the John Day Fossil Beds are dedicated to preserving the resources for generations to come.

420 West Main Street
John Day, OR 97845
(800) 523-1235, or
  (503) 987-2333

Admission: Low fee

Facilities: Rest rooms, gift shop, wheelchair accessible

CURATOR'S CORNER

TED FREMD

Paleontologist
John Day Fossil Beds National Monument

"The John Day Fossil Beds National Monument consists of three different geographically separate areas or 'units': Sheep Rock, Painted Hills, and Clarno," Mr. Fremd explains. "Among the three of them, over 40 million years are chronicled. With climates shifting from paratropical to a cool, high desert, the diversity of the plant and animal fossils represented in this fossil record is very large. There are several trails, a visitor center, and research facilities at the monument.

"The opportunity to perceive and work with the ecosystems against a backdrop of such 'deep time' is tremendously rewarding. Discovering, uncovering, and curating new specimens into public repositories is always of interest. But it is the analyses of the biotas [the plants and animals of a region] on a grander scale that is most inspiring."

PENNSYLVANIA

ACADEMY OF NATURAL SCIENCE MUSEUM

So many outstanding dinosaur exhibits grace these historic halls that it would be tough to list them all in a limited space. But considering that this is one of the oldest museums in the United States, it has had a lot of time to collect fossil specimens. Included are fourteen complete life-size skeletons (*Tyrannosaurus rex* is just one), nests, hatchlings, footprints (one you can crawl into)—even an animated *Apatosaurus* and the marine reptile *Elasmosaurus*. The Academy of Natural Science Museum is one of the best places in the country to study dinosaurs, and more.

1900 Benjamin
  Franklin Parkway
Philadelphia, PA
  19103-1195
(215) 299-1000

Admission: Low fee

Facilities: Rest rooms, gift shop, food available, wheelchair accessible

WAGNER FREE INSTITUTE OF SCIENCE

Dinosaur bones are on display, but this museum's most unique feature is its Victorian architecture and interior design. With displays organized in a manner common among museums of the nineteenth century (it originally opened in 1865), it is not only a place to examine ancient fossils, but a special opportunity to see how those treasures were exhibited in days gone by.

17th Street and
  Montgomery Avenue
Philadelphia, PA 19121
(215) 763-6529

Admission: Low fee

Facilities: Rest rooms, gift shop, wheelchair accessible

THE CARNEGIE MUSEUM OF NATURAL HISTORY

Eleven different dinosaur skeletons are on display at this very famous museum, including *Allosaurus*, *Stegosaurus*, *Diplodocus*, *Apatosaurus*, and *Tyrannosaurus rex*. Other prehistoric animals are also on display, including ancient mammals, marine reptiles and pterosaurs.

4400 Forbes Avenue
Pittsburgh, PA
  15213-4080
(412) 622-3131

Admission: Low fee

Facilities: Rest rooms, gift shop, wheelchair accessible

CURATOR'S CORNER

ANDREW D. REDLINE, M.SC.

Research Assistant
Carnegie Museum of Natural History

"Every year, many young, aspiring paleontologists write to ask me what the proper steps are to becoming a professional in the field," says Mr. Redline. "Answering these inquiries is one of my primary pleasures, and illustrates what I believe the job is all about. The following are excerpts from one of my replies:

"*The best way to become a paleontologist is simple—decide that you already are one.* This may seem dumb, but it helps open the door to the work that will follow. If you are really cut out to be a paleontologist, it won't seem like work. You will be surprised to learn what is possible when you're interested in the topic. Most paleontologists will admit that they have done much of their training on their own.

"*Being a paleontologist means being a detective of earth history.* All evidence bearing on past life must be considered. Anatomy and physiology are critical to understanding animal structure and relationships. Genetics and embryology help in unraveling the evolutionary process. Geology and chemistry help in understanding the material basis and environmental context of the earth and its history of life. Even astronomy will help. The Earth is a product of the distribution of mass and energy in the universe. And what is possible on this

planet is a function of these relationships. Don't just study or read about dinosaurs.

"The last and most important point is, *Be interested in everything alive.* The true paleontologist pictures extinct life at the time when it was living. Notice how insects, birds, and flatworms live and relate to each other. How are they similar? How are they different? Why do the very closely related coyotes and wolves live in different areas and have different social structures? How do clams have babies? Why does this work in the marine environment?

"Nothing exists without its relationship to all that is around it, and to what has come before. This includes those objects of popular worship—the dinosaurs. They were living animals— probably unique in comparison to the animals we know today. But nevertheless, they were subject to the same rules and limitations. The knowledge of anything specific is impossible without the comparative bigger picture.

"Earth history is a wonderful subject that will never be told in its entirety. The fun is in the wondering—not in the knowing. If that makes sense to you, then you will probably be a good paleontologist. Good luck!"

RHODE ISLAND

HUDSON, FULLER, ST. PIERRE & CHASE COLLECTION OF RHODE ISLAND

 This collection's name makes it look more like a law firm than a museum, because several smaller collections were pooled together, and all of the names were kept. Most of what is on display reflects the region's ancient native peoples. But some prehistoric mammals are also included in fossil form.

Rhode Island College
600 Mount Pleasant
  Avenue
Providence, RI 02908
(401) 274-9774, or
  (401) 456-8005

Admission: Donation requested

Facilities: Rest rooms, food available, wheelchair accessible

ROCKS, MINERALS, FOSSILS

 A small teaching collection of fossils, including those of prehistoric plants and mammals, is on display for university students and the general public to explore.

University of Rhode
  Island
Geology Department
South Kingston, RI
(401) 792-2265

Admission: Free

Facilities: Rest rooms, food available, wheelchair accessible

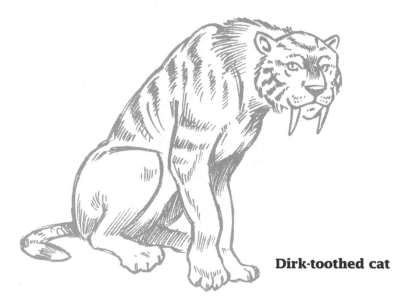

Dirk-toothed cat

SOUTH CAROLINA

CHARLESTON MUSEUM

The fossil resources here are well worth seeing, although the museum is considered an all-around museum of South Carolina history. According to experts, this museum has the largest collection of Oligocene whales. The second-largest *Pseudodontorn* (an early pelican-like bird) is on display here, complete with rare, toothlike projections in its beak. Also on display is an exhibit on the only Paleocene mammals found between the Rocky Mountains and the Eastern seaboard. Paleocene vertebrate fossil beds are extremely rare, according to the museum's curator of vertebrate paleontology, Dr. Albert E. Sanders (see Curator's Corner).

360 Meeting Street
Charleston, SC 29403
(803) 722-2996

Admission: Donation requested

Facilities: Rest rooms, gift shop, wheelchair accessible

SOUTH CAROLINA STATE MUSEUM

Like the Charleston Museum, this museum exhibits comprehensive material on South Carolina state history, but fossil history is a part of that information. Don't miss the exhibit on the country's latest laser technology.

301 Gervais Street
Columbia, SC 29201
(803) 737-4921

Admission: Donation requested

Facilities: Rest rooms, gift shop, wheelchair accessible

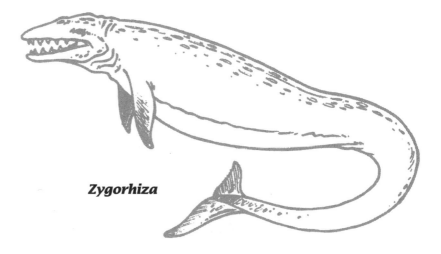

Zygorhiza

CURATOR'S CORNER

DR. ALBERT E. SANDERS

Curator of Natural Science
Charleston Museum

"A short time ago, a man and his son brought a fossil into my office for identification," Dr. Sanders remembers. "As I was showing them some of the fossils in the preparation area, the man suddenly said, 'You know, you have the best job in the world.' 'Yes, I suppose I do,' I replied.

"This is not to say that there are no disappointments or frustrations in paleontology. Every profession has its share of ups and downs. But the excitement that one experiences in the discovery of new additions to the fossil record of a region more than makes up for any aggravations encountered along the way. When we excavate a new specimen, I am still impressed by the fact that as we slowly remove the dirt from around the bones, it is the first time that they have seen the light of day in millions of years. Ours are the first human eyes ever to have seen them.

"None of the many professional paleontologists that I know and work with has any regrets about entering that field, and I'm quite certain that virtually all of them would be dreadfully unhappy if, for some reason, they suddenly had to give up their abiding interest in fossils. If you are willing to obtain the proper education, I would say, 'Do it!' You'll never get rich, but you certainly won't starve, either. There are many ways to measure wealth. Because I am doing the work that I most enjoy, I consider myself to be as rich as any man on Earth."

SOUTH DAKOTA

FLINTSTONE'S BEDROCK CITY

Fred and Barney welcome you to their own official "Stone Age" amusement park, complete with "Mount Rockmore" (remarkably similar to South Dakota's world-famous landmark, Mount Rushmore) and Dino Dogs (a.k.a. hot dogs). Don't expect a single scientific offering or dinosaur fossils, but instead a fantasy adventure in a prehistoric setting that could only exist in creative human minds. With that in mind, you won't be disappointed.

P.O. Box 649
Custer, SD 57730
(605) 673-4079

Admission: Moderate fee

Facilities: Rest rooms, gift shop, food available, wheelchair accessible

MAMMOTH SITE OF HOT SPRINGS

Hundreds of woolly mammoths met their deaths here by way of a slippery sinkhole in what would become Hot Springs, South Dakota, leaving behind a mass bone bed. Today, in late June through July, visitors can join expert paleontologists in exploring the secrets left behind by these Ice Age elephants, or examine previously excavated exhibit material throughout the balance of the year. There is a well-appointed visitor center.

P.O. Box 606
Hot Springs, SD 57747
(605) 745 6017

Admission: Low fee

Facilities: Rest rooms, gift shop, food available, wheelchair accessible

BADLANDS NATIONAL PARK

A varied collection of fossils, ranging from ancient mammalian giants to tiny prehistoric mice, is on display in the visitor center here. But because a great many fossil resources have yet to be excavated, on any given summer day you can see paleo experts working as you explore the park. In fact, the resources are so rich that the National Park Service has been urged to hire a paleontologist to care for the fossils, though that has not happened thus far.

P.O. Box 6
Interior, SD 57750
(605) 433-5362

Admission: Low fee

Facilities: Rest rooms, gift shop, wheelchair accessible

BLACK HILLS INSTITUTE OF GEOLOGICAL RESEARCH

In August of 1990, Black Hills Institute volunteer Sue Hendrickson stumbled across a fossil find that would rock any paleontologist's world, though neither she nor BHI founder and president Peter Larson knew at the time just what the find was. The Institute paid the landowner $5,000 to collect the specimen. This time the roll of the dice seemed to pay off. Hendrickson had found "Sue," the most complete *T. rex* ever discovered.

But because the landowner was Native American—Lakota Sioux—his ranch land and all mineral and fossil rights on that acreage were held in trust by the United States government. Concerned that the proper collection permits had not been issued, the FBI raided the Black Hills Institute two years later, and took Sue away. Many BHI opponents applauded the confiscation, fearing that the commercial fossil organization would sell the skeleton to the highest bidder. But Larson and his associates in fact planned to keep the amazing skeleton in the Institute museum in Hill City.

Court officials denied Peter Larson and the Black Hills Institute's rights to Sue. She is currently in storage at the South Dakota School of Mines, and will likely be awarded to the ranch owner, who is, ironically, expected to sell the amazing *T. rex* to the highest bidder.

Such controversy has overshadowed the incredible work at the Black Hills Institute. But travelers can visit the fossil lab and museum, explore the remarkable fossil resources for sale and on display, often meet members of the Larson family, and decide for themselves where they stand on the debate.

217 Main Street
P.O. Box 643
Hill City, SD 57745
(605) 574-4289

Admission: Low fee

Facilities: Rest rooms, gift shop, wheelchair accessible

DINOSAUR PARK

This park, complete with picnic facilities, features five life-size (roughly) concrete dinosaur models, including *T. rex*, *Stegosaurus*, *Apatosaurus*, and an unspecified duckbill. It's not true science, but it offers a unique photo opportunity to visitors. Because the dinosaurs are made of a durable material, some climbing is allowed. So while kids of all ages shimmy up the nonscientific reproductions, their faithful family photographers can capture each "Kodak moment."

3223 Stockade
Rapid City, SD 57702
(605) 343-8687

Admission: Low fee

Facilities: Rest rooms, gift shop, food available, wheelchair accessible

MUSEUM OF GEOLOGY

Edmontosaurus, marine reptiles including plesiosaurs and mosasaurs, and a good cross-section of prehistoric mammals are on exhibit here. But in recent years the university has become well known for keeping "Sue," the most complete *Tyrannosaurus rex* skeleton ever collected, in cold storage while the FBI decides her ultimate fate. Actually, some say Sue is not on ice, but rather crated up in a hot, damp boiler room—a dangerous place for so fragile a resource. But with any luck, she'll soon get the respect and preparation she deserves.

South Dakota School
  of Mines
500 East St. Joseph
  Street
Rapid City, SD 57701
(605) 394-2467

Admission: Donation requested

Facilities: Rest rooms, gift shop, food available

WALL DRUG DINOSAUR

This eighty-foot giant, which stands outside the famous Wall Drug store, is more Americana than science, dating back more than fifty years. But the bright green sauropod—referred to as a *Brontosaurus* (the creature now known as *Apatosaurus*)—started out as a marketing draw for an ordinary drugstore. Now it's a popular stop for tourists and locals, featuring a gas station, a gift shop, a restaurant, and a museum. The museum gives a history of the drugstore and the town, including how the dinosaur was built.

510 Main Street
Wall, SD 57790
(605) 279-2175

Admission: Low fee

Facilities: Rest rooms, gift shop, food available, wheelchair accessible

Edmontosaurus

CURATOR'S CORNER

KRISTIN DONNAN

Freelance Writer

"Saddling up the parents for a ride back in time?" Ms. Donnan asks. "Certainly you will want to follow the 'tracks' of scientists over the years—footsteps that will lead you to visit the Great Plains, one of the most prolific fossil areas in the country. If a prehistoric trip is in the works, there should be a law against missing South Dakota."

"South Dakota is a geological and paleontological textbook, where virtually all ages of rocks—from 2.5 billion to just 10,000 years old—are preserved,' explains Peter Larson, president of the Black Hills Institute of Geological Research. 'If you drive from the center of the Black Hills east across the prairie, you travel from near the beginning of life up to the present!'

"The Black Hills Institute, located in Hill City, is the largest freelance fossil preparatory in the world. Fossils discovered, prepared, and mounted by Institute scientists are sold to museums and collections all over the world. They also have their own museum—the Black Hills Museum of Natural History—where fossil *Tyrannosaurus rex*, duckbills, *Triceratops*, "bird-mimic" dinosaurs, and other species are being readied for display. Visitors will be able to view short- and long-necked plesiosaurs, mosasaurs, the longest Cretaceous fish

found to date (eighteen feet long), fossil plants, ammonites, and more.

"The Institute supports itself through selling what are considered plentiful fossils. However, Institute paleontologists are involved in many research projects—including Peter Larson's research into dinosaur sexual dimorphism (skeletal differences that indicate gender). Brand-new information is being gathered from one of the *T. rex* skeleton's teeth, and Institute CT scans and hands-on studies of fossil dinosaur eggs have revealed dinosaur embryos.

"South Dakota children benefit from this fossil frenzy with "Dinosaurs on Wheels," a traveling educational outreach program that takes Institute dinosaurs and paleontologists to schools for special interactive exhibits.

"The Institute is also on the cutting edge of fossil politics, with a battle over the custody of the biggest and most complete *Tyrannosaurus rex* ever discovered, named "Sue." She, too, was found in South Dakota.

"See you in South Dakota! Make sure you bring bug spray, boots, sun screen, a hat, a canteen, and a backpack with plenty of room for fossils and fun! Oh, and watch out for snakes and ticks . . . and *T. rex*."

TENNESSEE

COON CREEK SCIENCE CENTER

Paleontological exhibits from the seventy-million-year-old Coon Creek Fossil Formation are on display at this educational center, open to visitors only by advance reservation. In fact, very few organizations are allowed access to the Coon Creek Science Center, apart from local school districts, because this is not a museum but an education outreach featuring residential cabins, a dining hall, and in-depth fossil camps where students learn to collect, identify, and prepare Tennessee fossil resources. Call in advance for information on group visits.

Coon Creek Farm
Route 2, P.O. Box 540
Adamsville, TN 39310
(901) 632-4850

Admission: Moderate fee

Facilities: Rest rooms, food available, wheelchair accessible

HANDS ON! REGIONAL MUSEUM

The museum mascot is a friendly *Tyrannosaurus rex*, but the museum does not yet feature a full-time dinosaur exhibit. There are plans to add a prehistoric exhibit, however, and traveling dinosaur tours are regularly booked, so call ahead for schedule information.

315 East Main Street
Johnson City, TN 37601
(615) 434-HAND

Admission: Low fee

Facilities: Rest rooms, gift shop, wheelchair accessible

EAST TENNESSEE DISCOVERY CENTER

This museum offers a good cross-section of local fossils, and has exhibits on other aspects of prehistoric life in ancient Tennessee as well as other displays of general interest.

516 North Beaman Street
Knoxville, TN 37914
(615) 637-1121

Admission: Donation requested

Facilities: Rest rooms, gift shop, wheelchair accessible

FRANK H. MCCLUNG MUSEUM

 There is not a great deal of paleontology explored at this archaeology museum, but it does feature dinosaur tracks and a few Ice Age mammals, including a saber-toothed cat and an armadillo-like *Glyptodon*.

University of Tennessee
1327 Circle Park Drive
Knoxville, TN 37996-3200
(615) 974-2144

Admission: Donation requested

Facilities: Rest rooms, gift shop, food available, wheelchair accessible

MEMPHIS PINK PALACE MUSEUM

 This museum's prehistoric exhibit, "Geology: 4.6 Billion Years of Earth History," is likely one of Tennessee's best, featuring not only dinosaur tracks, but a mastodon skeletal cast, a full mosasaur skeleton, and a life-size *Dilophosaurus* model. Special exhibits on marine invertebrate fossils and other natural-science topics also form part of this impressive museum's offering.

3050 Central Avenue
Memphis, TN 38111-3399
(901) 320-6320

Admission: Low fee

Facilities: Rest rooms, gift shop, food available, wheelchair accessible

TENNESSEE RIVER MUSEUM

A small exhibit of fossils native to Tennessee are part of this museum's natural-science offering.

c/o Chamber of Commerce
507 Main Street
Savannah, TN 38372
(800) 552-FUNN

Admission: Donation requested

Facilities: Rest rooms, gift shop, wheelchair accessible

Glyptodon

CURATOR'S CORNER

BOBBY KING

Paleontologist
Coon Creek Science Center

"I have always been intrigued by Earth's prehistoric life," claims Mr. King. "And the only means we have of studying that life is through a detailed examination of the fossil record. Through the study, we are given a window into Earth's ancient history itself.

"The pinnacle of my career with the Coon Creek Science Center came in November 1990, as staff from our center and the Memphis Pink Palace Museum excavated the partial skeletal remains of a mosasaur. To see the ancient swimming reptile slowly uncovered and moved from its 70-million-year-old resting place is beyond description. This creature, at the top of the food chain, roamed western Tennessee during the late Cretaceous period.

"Just as exciting, but in a different way, is the unique opportunity I have to share my experiences with the students who visit our center. To see their excitement and to help kindle the flame of curiosity in these young minds is compensation enough for the work I do. And my advice to them is always the same: Dare to dream, and then nurture your dreams with diligent study and hard work. That is my advice to you, too!"

TEXAS

TEXAS MEMORIAL MUSEUM

Some say the housing is not up to the quality of the fossil collection, which is all the more reason to visit the museum, donations in hand. But you will definitely get what you pay for, considering that one of the largest flying reptiles ever found is represented by a *Quetzalcoatlus* wing impression discovered by a University of Texas student at Big Bend National Park. It indicates that the pterosaur had a fifty-foot wingspan. Also on display are various fossilized bones from *Diplodocus* and from reptiles and amphibians that predate the dinosaurs—such as *Eryops* and *Dimetrodon*—as well as from Ice Age mammals.

University of Texas
2400 Trinity Street
Austin, TX 78705
(512) 471-1604

Admission: Donation requested

Facilities: Rest rooms, gift shop, food available, wheelchair accessible

BIG BEND NATIONAL PARK

A cast of the same giant *Quetzalcoatlus* exhibited at the Texas Memorial Museum is on display in the Big Bend National Park visitor center. It was discovered in the park in 1971 by a University of Texas graduate student. Smaller specimens have been found in the park since then, but none to equal the fifty-foot king. A word to the wise: the territory is rugged at Big Bend, so if you want to hike the park, be prepared for a challenge. As always, do not collect fossils on federal land without permits, and do not collect on private land without written permission from the owner.

Big Bend National Park, TX 79834
(915) 477-2251

Admission: Low fee

Facilities: Rest rooms, gift shop, wheelchair accessible

PANHANDLE PLAINS HISTORICAL MUSEUM

The city of Canyon is a lovely setting for this small museum of local history. The breathtaking geology of the area will explain why fossils are a significant part of the museum's exhibits.

2401 Fourth Avenue
Canyon, TX 79015
(806) 656-2244

Admission: Donation requested

Facilities: Rest rooms, gift shop, wheelchair accessible

CORPUS CHRISTI MUSEUM OF SCIENCE AND HISTORY

 This museum's paleontology hall is organized as a children's exhibit and includes a *T. rex* skull replica as well as a dinosaur nest, dinosaur track casts, a *Pteranodon* model, and a full skeletal cast of a mosasaur, a marine reptile.

1900 North Chaparral
Corpus Christi, TX
 78401
(512) 883-2862

Admission: Low fee

Facilities: Rest rooms, gift shop, wheelchair accessible

DALLAS MUSEUM OF NATURAL HISTORY

Tenontosaurus was a species common to Texas 115 million years ago. It is exhibited at this Dallas museum along with a thirty-one-foot-long mosasaur, a large ancient sea turtle and a good collection of Ice Age mammals in the museum's Prehistoric Texas Hall.

P.O. Box 26193
Dallas, TX 75226
(214) 670-8457

Admission: Low fee

Facilities: Rest rooms, gift shop, wheelchair accessible

CURATOR'S CORNER

DR. LOUIS JACOBS

Director, Shuler Museum of Paleontology
Southern Methodist University

"I started out studying mammals without much concern for dinosaurs," says Dr. Jacobs. "Because dinosaurs are so popular, I thought everything was known about them. I was wrong. While searching for mammals, I found dinosaurs instead. In the process, I learned that much is left to be discovered about the creatures who ruled the land during the Age of Reptiles. Exciting finds can still be made.

"Fossils of all kinds help us to understand the relationship between the Earth and the life on it. The Earth is dynamic. It has changed throughout its history because of drifting continents, changing environments, and evolving life. That is why fossils found in one place are so important to understanding fossils found in other places.

"Paleontology shows us the common history that all life shares. It allows us to understand how the Earth got to be the way it is. Knowing the past helps us to anticipate the future. Why is that important? Here is one reason: Environmental problems that humans themselves can cause are the same ones that dinosaurs faced from volcanoes or asteroids. They are the natural experiments that we can learn from now."

THE SCIENCE PLACE

Three animated dinosaur models are on display at this family-oriented museum: a *Tyrannosaurus rex* and a mother *Apatosaurus* and her hatchling. Though these are the only permanent prehistoric displays, Dinamation International exhibits are frequently featured, as are other fossil exhibits on loan from museums across the state and country. Call ahead for up-to-the-minute information.

P.O. Box 151469
Dallas, TX 75315
(214) 428-7200

Admission: Low fee

Facilities: Rest rooms, gift shop, wheelchair accessible

SHULER MUSEUM OF PALEONTOLOGY

Dr. Louis Jacobs, a world-famous paleontologist, is this museum's director. He has written books on the dinosaurs of Texas as well as on fossil finds he's studied in Africa. When you visit the Shuler Museum, you'll be able to examine much of his work firsthand.

Southern Methodist
  University
Department of
  Geological Science
Dallas, TX 75275-0395
(214) 768-2000

Admission: Donation requested

Facilities: Rest rooms, gift shop, wheelchair accessible

FORT WORTH MUSEUM OF SCIENCE & HISTORY

The Texas native dinosaur *Tenontosaurus* is highlighted here, but it is just the start of many paleo exhibits at this exciting, innovative museum. One of the most unusual interactive offerings is the DinoDig—an actual replica of the Doss Ranch bone beds that yielded several nearly complete *Tenontosaurus* skeletons. Dinosaur fans of all ages can get a taste of real-life paleontology without suffering the rugged conditions professionals face. Life-size dinosaur restoration models are also on full-time display, along with popular traveling dinosaur exhibits.

1501 Montgomery Street
Fort Worth, TX 76107
(817) 732-1631

Admission: Low fee

Facilities: Rest rooms, gift shop, food available, wheelchair accessible

DINOSAUR VALLEY STATE PARK

At this site, now a state park, a little girl discovered large tracks along the banks of the Paluxy River in 1909. Relatives insisted they were markings left behind by Native Americans, but she didn't believe a word of it. Roland T. Bird, a dinosaur expert, confirmed her suspicions in 1938 when he declared that these were in fact dinosaur tracks nearly 100 million years old. Now you, too, can see the tracks at this state park. Tracks from sauropods (such as *Apatosaurus*) and from bipedal plant-eaters and carnivores are well represented. And two dinosaur models from the 1964 New York World's Fair were donated to the state park by the Atlantic Richfield Company in 1970—*Tyrannosaurus rex* and *Apatosaurus*.

P.O. Box 396
Glen Rose, TX 78043
(817) 897-4588

Admission: Low fee

Facilities: Rest rooms, gift shop

DINOSAUR TRACKS

Located in a riverbed on private property about twenty-two miles from the city of Hondo, these tracks are considered outstanding specimens and are clearly visible to professionals or amateurs. Call the Chamber of Commerce for directions. The landowners welcome visitors and accept donations via a tin can wired to a nearby fencepost.

c/o Chamber of
  Commerce
P.O. Box 126
Hondo, TX 78861
(210) 426-3037

Admission: Donation requested

Facilities: None

HOUSTON NATURAL SCIENCE MUSEUM

Seventy feet of *Diplodocus* skeleton greets you as you enter this museum's main hall. Other models surround him. But the museum is not limited to paleo resources. In addition to life-like shark models that seem to swim through the air above the hall, prehistoric mammals such as *Dinictis felina* (a saber-toothed cat) and *Mesohippus* (an ancient horse) are on display. Space, minerals, medicine, and petroleum are also well represented.

One Houston Circle
  Drive
Houston, TX 77030
(713) 639-4600

Admission: Low fee

Facilities: Rest rooms, gift shop, wheelchair accessible

ROBERT A. VINES ENVIRONMENTAL SCIENCE CENTER

The geology hall at this center houses a number of high-profile dinosaur fossils including an *Allosaurus* skeleton thirty-three feet long, a skull cast of *Tyrannosaurus rex* and casts or copies of *Apatosaurus* tracks.

8856 Westview Drive
Houston, TX 77055
(713) 465-9628

Admission: Low fee

Facilities: Rest rooms, gift shop, wheelchair accessible

BRAZOSPORT MUSEUM OF NATURAL SCIENCE

The museum is primarily known for its large collection of shells. Fossils are the secondary exhibit, but it's a hard call to make. A twenty-five-foot *Allosaurus* skeleton heads up the fossil exhibit. In fact, this museum offers a unique identification service for both fossils and shells.

400 College Drive
Lake Jackson, TX 77566
(409) 265-7831

Admission: Donation requested

Facilities: Rest rooms, gift shop, wheelchair accessible

MUSEUM OF TEXAS TECH UNIVERSITY

Famous for their Ranching Heritage Center, created to honor the historical contributions of the cattle industry, this museum also exhibits animals of more ancient origin. An *Allosaurus* replica is on hand, as well as bits and pieces from other dinosaur species. Ice Age mammals (including the skull of a Columbian mammoth) are also displayed.

Fourth and Indiana
Lubbock, TX 79409
(806) 742-2490

Admission: Donation requested

Facilities: Rest rooms, gift shop, wheelchair accessible

HEARD NATURAL SCIENCE MUSEUM

A skull from a mosasaur (*Tylosaurus*) is on display here, along with other local fossils. This museum also doubles as a wildlife sanctuary. Its founder, Bessie Heard, hoped to preserve a part of Texas that she held dear as a child, to honor both her family and children yet to come.

One Nature Place
McKinney, TX 75069
(214) 562-5566

Admission: Low fee

Facilities: Rest rooms, gift shop, wheelchair accessible

DINOSAUR GARDENS

This collection of Texas dinosaurs is more attraction than museum. But it offers a worthwhile collection of tracks, skeletons and models. Some have animated features. Each has an explanatory marker.

P.O. Box 98
Moscow, TX 75960
(409) 398-4565

Admission: Low fee

Facilities: Rest rooms, gift shop, wheelchair accessible

WITTE MUSEUM OF HISTORY AND SCIENCE

A complete *Triceratops* skeleton is on on display in the lobby of this museum. Other fossil exhibits have been featured from time to time, on a temporary basis. Call in advance for details.

3801 Broadway
San Antonio, TX 78209
(210) 820-2111

Admission: Low fee

Facilities: Rest rooms, gift shop, wheelchair accessible

DINOSAUR FLATS

Hundreds of three-toed dinosaur tracks were discovered at this site just over ten years ago. Put down 100 million years earlier, when the region was a saltwater marsh, the tracks have not yet been positively identified. This is a private residence, and the owners closed it to all but children's educational groups in 1995. However, those groups can not only see the tracks but dig for marine fossils, thanks to the generosity of the landowners.

4831 FM 2673
Canyon Lake, TX 78133
(210) 899-7431

Admission: Donation requested

Facilities: Rest rooms, gift shop

STRECKER MUSEUM

Acrocanthosaurus tracks from the Glen Rose region were removed and sold via roadside vendors in the 1930s. Many have since been donated to this small museum, and are on display along with a twelve-foot *Protostega* (an ancient sea turtle) and an unidentified plesiosaur found at the Lake Waco dam.

South Fourth and
  Speight
P.O. Box 97154
Waco, TX 76798
(817) 755-1110

Admission: Donation requested

Facilities: Rest rooms, gift shop, wheelchair accessible

CURATOR'S CORNER

DR. JAMES F. DIFFILY

Director of Collections and Exhibits
Fort Worth Museum of Science and History

"Dinosaurs lived—and became extinct—millions of years before humans appeared on the earth. Yet in books, on films, and in museum displays, we see fully fleshed dinosaurs interacting with each other and the environment. How do we know what their world was like?" Dr. Diffily asks.

"We have some idea because a dinosaur fossil site contains much more than just fossilized bones. By carefully studying the rocks and other fossils found there, we can discover things about the environment and the community in which dinosaurs lived.

"The Doss Ranch site in Parker County, Texas—excavated by the Fort Worth Museum of Science and History in 1989—tells such a story. About 113 million years ago, three *Tenontosaurus* dinosaurs died and their bodies ended up in a shallow lagoon. How do we know this? The types of rock and the presence of fish and oyster fossils at the Doss Ranch site tell us. Later, fossil evidence shows that a system of sluggish streams moved over the lagoon, carrying logs from a nearby conifer forest. The logs—which turned to coal—fossil pollen, and stream-channel deposits tell this part of the story. Finally, fossil-rich layers of limestone at the site tell of a shallow tropical sea that later moved in over the land.

"Each new fossil find adds to our understanding of the world's rich history. Keep looking—the *Tenontosaurus* site described above was found by an eight-year-old boy. Your find could add another piece to the puzzle. If you do find something, call a local museum or university."

UTAH

MUSEUM OF THE SAN RAFAEL

 Because dinosaurs are so much a part of local history in this region, this county museum includes a good paleontology display. A complete skeletal replica of *Allosaurus* is the pride of the museum, but other fossils are exhibited as well.

96 North 100 East
Castle Dale, UT 84513
(801) 381-5252

Admission: Donation requested

Facilities: Rest rooms, gift shop, wheelchair accessible

ESCALANTE PETRIFIED FOREST

 This petrified forest, located one mile west of Escalante, is from the Jurassic Morrison Formation, 60 to 70 million years younger than Arizona's Petrified Forest (remains from a Triassic forest). A visitor center and well-marked interpretive trail help direct your fossil exploration. Call for specific directions.

P.O. Box 350
Escalante, UT 84726
(801) 826-4466

Admission: Low fee

Facilities: Rest rooms, gift shop

DINOSAUR NATIONAL MONUMENT

If you have time to visit only one Utah fossil stop, this national monument should be your choice. World-famous as one of the richest dinosaur bone beds ever discovered, it provides an opportunity to explore fossil remains of nine different species (so far) in a single location. In fact, the excavation work is ongoing, with professional paleontologists working as you watch. A year-round visitor center actually houses the dig, still embedded in the Utah mountainside.

P.O. Box 128
Jensen, UT 84035
(801) 789-2115

Admission: Low fee

Facilities: Rest rooms, gift shop, food available, wheelchair accessible

CURATOR'S CORNER

DR. DAVID D. GILLETTE

Utah State Paleontologist

"I'm still trying to catch up with all of those paleontologists who knew as children that they wanted to grow up and study fossils," Dr. Gillette says. "I was always told I would be an 'engineer,' and was truly disappointed later in life to learn that being an engineer was not the same as driving a freight train.

"My first contact with fossils was when I was a first-grader in Indiana. We played in the gravel beneath the swing sets and mindlessly collected little handfuls of 'Indian Beads' that we strung together as necklaces for our mothers. These were actually the stems of crinoids or 'sea lilies' from ancient seas of the Midwest, more than 400 million years old. I was astonished as a student in my first course in paleontology to learn that the Indian beads of my youth were actually the parts of long-extinct animals.

"Paleontology, for me, is a substitute for my childhood dreams of becoming a cowboy. I work out west in the canyons and deserts. I sleep under the stars and hear coyotes at night. I work hard in the hot sun. I brand (label) our critters (fossils), and hold roundups (collecting expeditions), and I am close to the natural world."

MILL CANYON DINOSAUR TRAIL

This quarter-mile self-guided trail contains the tracks of many dinosaurs, including *Allosaurus*, *Camptosaurus*, *Stegosaurus*, and *Camarasaurus*. You'll find maps in a box at the start of the trail, and there are markers along the way to guide visitors. Call the Bureau of Land Management at the number listed for more details. The sign at the beginning of the tour reads, "There are no guards or fences here. You are the protectors of this valuable resource. Only you can assure that this fragile legacy is preserved." But Utah state and federal Bureau of Land Management authorities know and patrol the territory on a regular basis. Fossil theft will not be tolerated.

Highway 191
Mile Marker 141
 Turnoff
(13 miles north of Moab)
Moab, UT 54532
(801) 259-7814

Admission: Donation requested

Facilities: None

SAUROPOD DINOSAUR TRACKSITE

Like Mill Canyon, these dinosaur tracks are at remote locations without interpretive visitor centers or regular staffing. Visitors are welcome—the Bureau of Land Management will hand out detailed directions upon request. But, as at Mill Canyon, the trails are well patrolled, and theft will be dealt with harshly.

Potash Road Dinosaur Tracks
c/o Grand Resource Area Bureau of Land Management
885 South Sand Flats Road
Moab, UT 84532
(801) 359-8193

Admission: Donation requested

Facilities: None

DAN O'LAURIE MUSEUM

This small-town museum of local history includes some fossil material, because prehistoric animals are a big part of Utah's ancient legacy. Included are dinosaur-track castings and a few small fossils.

118 East Center Street
Moab, UT 84532
(801) 259-7985

Admission: Donation requested

Facilities: Rest rooms, wheelchair accessible

DEAD HORSE POINT STATE PARK

The visitor center at this state park is, in fact, a museum with displays of ancient plants and animals, including dinosaurs. The lives and lifestyles of ancient peoples are also explored. Park rangers offer educational programs on most of the topics listed.

P.O. Box 609
Moab, UT 84532-0609
(801) 259-6511

Admission: Low fee

Facilities: Rest rooms, gift shop, wheelchair accessible

THE DINOSAUR MUSEUM

Steven and Sylvia Czerkas are well known in the world of dinosaur publishing and fine art. With luck and a lot of very hard work, they will add museum curatorship to their already impressive dinosaur credentials in the summer of 1995, when they hope to open their museum. Expect state-of-the-art dinosaur reconstruction models including an *Apatosaurus*, reflecting the latest exciting theory. Fossil evidence suggests that this sauropod may have had a series of bony spikes protruding from its back.

754 South 200 West
Blanding, UT 84511
(no phone yet available)

Admission: Low fee

Facilities: Rest rooms, gift shop, wheelchair accessible

GEORGE S. ECCLES DINOSAUR PARK

 The city of Ogden donated the use of fifty acres of riverside land for this outdoor dinosaur preserve. The prehistoric residents are actually lifelike models (more than fifty so far, with yet more on the way) by the Arizona Larson Company. Most are strictly "hands off," but there is a sand pit with a life-size, climbable *Ankylosaurus* and other fossil-themed play features.

1544 East Park
  Boulevard
Ogden, UT 84401
(801) 393-3466, or
  (801) 626-6339

Admission: Low fee

Facilities: Rest rooms, gift shop, wheelchair accessible

MUSEUM OF NATURAL SCIENCE

 Dimetrodon, a sail-backed prehistoric reptile often mistaken for a dinosaur, is on display at this museum, along with skeletal replicas of *Allosaurus* and *Apatosaurus*. A few ancient mammals are also exhibited.

Weber State University
Lind Lecture Hall
3705 Harrison
  Boulevard
Ogden, UT 84408
(801) 626-6653

Admission: Donation requested

Facilities: Rest rooms, wheelchair accessible

CLEVELAND-LLOYD DINOSAUR QUARRY

Discovered in 1928, this quarry has yielded more than 10,000 dinosaur bones. Even so, the find is so rich, it is still excavated by paleontologists today. Tours originate from the visitor center, guiding you through a dry area that was a shallow lake 150 million years ago. Most bones collected have been from *Allosaurus*, but many species were likely attracted to the lush, green habitat.

P.O. Drawer A.B.
Price, UT 84501
(801) 637-4584

Admission: Donation requested

Facilities: Rest rooms, gift shop, wheelchair accessible

PREHISTORIC MUSEUM

Once you've visited the active Cleveland Lloyd quarry (see above), visit the museum that houses much of the excavated fossil material here on this small college campus. "Al" the *Allosaurus* is exhibited along with skeletal mounts of *Stegosaurus*, *Camptosaurus*, and *Camarasaurus*. There are also dinosaur tracks recovered from a nearby coal mine.

College of Eastern Utah
155 East Main
Price, UT 84501
(801) 627-5060

Admission: Donation requested

Facilities: Rest rooms, gift shop, wheelchair accessible

EARTH SCIENCE MUSEUM

This science museum at Brigham Young University has a wealth of paleontology exhibits, including *Ultrasaurus* and *Supersaurus* bones—the largest dinosaur species yet discovered. But these are not the only paleo resources here. Visitors can watch fossil preparation in a working lab, and explore a series of exhibits including one on dinosaur embryos X-rayed inside ancient fossilized eggs. Paleo murals and skeletal mounts of *Allosaurus* and *Camptosaurus* round out the ever-growing collection.

Brigham Young University
1683 North Canyon Road
Provo, UT 84602
(801) 378-3680

Admission: Donation requested

Facilities: Rest rooms, food available, wheelchair accessible

WARNER VALLEY DINOSAUR TRACKSITE

Fort Pierce, an old military establishment, is the landmark nearest this very rural dinosaur track site. But finding the tracks without Bureau of Land Management directions would be next to impossible. So call ahead for hours, details, and specific directions.

c/o U.S. Bureau of Land Management
225 North Bluff Street
St. George, UT 84770
(801) 673-4654

Admission: Free

Facilities: Rest rooms (at BLM headquarters)

CURATOR'S CORNER

KENNETH L. STADTMAN

Curator, Earth Science Museum
Brigham Young University

"I had the opportunity to take a preparator's position with 'Dinosaur Jim' Jensen here at BYU in 1970," says Mr. Stadtman. "In 1972 a Jurassic Period dinosaur site in western Colorado called the Dry Mesa Quarry was begun as an excavation for the BYU Earth Science Museum. This site has produced not only the largest sauropod dinosaurs ever found, but an extremely varied range of other dinosaurs as well. Many of those found are new to science. Pterosaurs, crocodiles, and turtles were also found.

"We work at several other dinosaur sites, and have collected a number of interesting and rare dinosaurs. But because we continue to work at Dry Mesa, and because it has produced such a large variety of bones, it has certainly been the focus of my career at BYU. There is much work to be done, in preparation and research, on the specimens from this site. But it continues to be exciting, intriguing work."

THE DINO-TREKKING SITES

UTAH MUSEUM OF NATURAL HISTORY

This outstanding state museum is actually located on campus at the University of Utah. The diversity of its fossil collection is well known in the world of paleontology, owing in part to the dedicated efforts of Utah State paleontologist David D. Gillette. Featured are *Allosaurus*, *Barosaurus*, *Camptosaurus*, and *Stegosaurus* in full skeletal mounts. Other dinosaur species and prehistoric mammals are also represented in bits and pieces, or in full reconstructions.

University of Utah
President's Circle
Salt Lake City, UT
 84112
(801) 581-4303

Admission: Low fee

Facilities: Rest rooms, gift shop, wheelchair accessible

RED FLEET STATE PARK

Signs reading "CAUTION! DINOSAUR CROSSING!" mark the road near Red Fleet State Park—a quiet boast, considering that the park can lay claim to a good variety of dinosaur footprints or tracks. Some are very clearly defined, some are not so clear. But they seem to be from two different unidentified dinosaur species.

Steinaker Lake North
 4335
Vernal, UT 84078-9500
(801) 789-6614, or
 (801) 789-6630

Admission: Low fee

Facilities: Rest rooms, gift shop

UTAH FIELD HOUSE OF NATURAL HISTORY

A *Triceratops* peeks out of the bushes—all thirty feet of her. A six-ton *Stegosaurus* is only a few steps away. *Tyrannosaurus rex* is within sight, as are eleven more life-size, fleshed-out dinosaur sculptures in a garden setting so lush it all seems almost real. The models are well cared for, despite being outdoors year round, and are worth the stop on your way to Dinosaur National Monument (see entry on page 123). The museum adjacent to the garden houses more dinosaurian exhibits, as well as artifacts from more-modern Utah residents.

Dinosaur Gardens
235 East Main
Vernal, UT 84078
(801) 789-3799

Admission: Low fee

Facilities: Rest rooms, gift shop, wheelchair accessible

VERMONT

MONTSHIRE MUSEUM OF SCIENCE

Dinosaur fossils are not common in New England, but this museum has a few resources. Some are part of a larger reptile exhibit, for comparison purposes. A dinosaur thigh bone is part of a hands-on exhibit designed to give visitors an up-close look at museum treasures. But a great many paleo resources are waiting behind the scenes at Montshire for the funding necessary to prepare and display them properly. Call ahead to see how the prehistoric picture might have expanded. (See Curator's Corner.)

P.O. Box 770
Montshire Road
Norwich, VT 05055
(802) 649-2200

Admission: Low fee

Facilities: Rest rooms, gift shop, wheelchair accessible

FAIRBANKS MUSEUM AND PLANETARIUM

Although New England is not, for the most part, "dinosaur country," prehistoric fossils are a part of this museum's displays. But it is the planetarium for which Fairbanks is best known.

Main Street and
   Prospect
St. Johnsbury, VT
   05819
(802) 748-2372

Admission: Low

Facilities: Rest rooms, wheelchair accessible

CURATOR'S CORNER

JOAN WALTERMIRE

Curator
Montshire Museum of Science

"Our natural history collection came mostly from Dartmouth College and is one of the oldest college collections in the country," says Ms. Waltermire. "We are gradually putting it on display. The Montshire's founder was a mammalian paleontologist, so we have a good collection of fossil mammals, although they are not yet on exhibit.

"He was also a lover of kids, so we have some dinosaur bones, too. We have an entire *Apatosaurus* leg in plaster and burlap [fossils are often transported this way for protection, to keep them safe], waiting for restoration."

VIRGINIA

MUSEUM OF CULPEPER HISTORY

Revolutionary War artifacts make up the bulk of what this museum has to offer. But fossil evidence from the Culpeper Stone Quarry proves that dinosaurs roamed the land long before British and American soldiers.

140 East Davis Street
Culpeper, VA 22701
(703) 825-1973

Admission: Donation requested

Facilities: Rest rooms, gift shop

LURAY REPTILE CENTER AND DINOSAUR PARK

Though this site is primarily a petting zoo and a show-place for modern reptiles, several dinosaur models are also on display as a means of comparison and for all-around fun. Tropical bird shows are another good reason to make the stop a part of your travel plans. Most of the models are outside, but the shows and some exhibits are indoors.

Route 1, Box 481
Luray, VA 22835
(703) 743-4113

Admission: Low fee

Facilities: Rest rooms, gift shop, food available, wheelchair accessible

VIRGINIA MUSEUM OF NATURAL HISTORY

Unique at this museum is a computer-controlled *Triceratops* model. But there is also an excellent paleontological staff and an exhibit that reflects that expertise. Smaller models and a wealth of dinosaur-track castings are on display. The museum also sponsors, along with the Museum of Culpeper History, field trips to nearby trackways. It is expanding its paleontological displays to include an unidentified sauropod.

1001 Douglas Avenue
Martinville, VA 24122
(703) 666-8600

Admission: Donation requested

Facilities: Rest rooms, gift shop, wheelchair accessible

CURATOR'S CORNER

DR. NICHOLAS C. FRASER

Curator of Vertebrate Paleontology
Virginia Museum of Natural History

"Two unique sites in Virginia have paved the way for significant advances in our understanding of the evolution of land vertebrates," says Dr. Fraser. "One, near Richmond, has yielded remains of a mammal-like reptile that was previously considered largely restricted to the southern hemisphere. The second site contains exceptionally preserved plants, insects, fish, and reptiles. Among the insects are a number of very unusual forms that have not been previously described, including some of the world's first true flies. I consider this site comparable with the famous Solnhofen localities (of *Archaeopteryx* fame) in Germany, and it must rank among the most important fossil sites in North America."

ICE AGE MAMMAL DIG

It is important to note that this site is not yet a public exhibit, but an adults-only dig, sponsored by the Virginia Museum of Natural History, so all trips must be arranged through them. However, the dig has produced some exciting finds, including a set of giant sloth footprints—only the second set ever found in the United States. Write to inquire about community fossil displays in the near future.

c/o City Manager's
  Office
Saltville, VA 24307
(703) 496-5342

DINOSAUR LAND

This outdoor site is more Americana then science, but one of the very best of its kind. *Apatosaurus*, *Plateosaurus*, *Iguanodon*, *Triceratops*, *Corythosaurus*, *Moschops*, and *Tyrannosaurus rex* are represented here, along with twenty-three other larger-than-life models. Science is clearly not the main focus, but fun definitely is. King Kong and a sixty-foot shark join the saurian giants.

RFD 1, Box 63-A
White Post, VA 22663
(703) 869-2222

Admission: Low fee

Facilities: Rest rooms, gift shop, food available, wheelchair accessible

WASHINGTON

DRY FALLS INTERPRETIVE CENTER

A fossilized baby rhino preserved during the Ice Age may be seen here, and a life-size restoration model offers a detailed explanation of just how the young mammal might have died. This is a very special opportunity to study the lives of Ice Age mammals, on the site where they actually walked.

Sun Lakes Park
Coulee City, WA 99115
(509) 632-5214

Admission: Low fee

Facilities: Rest rooms, gift shop, wheelchair accessible

PAUL H. HARSHNER MEMORIAL MUSEUM

This is a small museum designed to educate and excite children about local history. A collection of fossils is just part of what is on display.

309 Fourth Street N.E.
Puyallup, WA 98372
(206) 841-8748

Admission: Donation requested

Facilities: Rest rooms, wheelchair accessible

PACIFIC SCIENCE CENTER

One of the Pacific Northwest's best dinosaur experiences, the Pacific Science Center offers a variety of dinosaur fossils, including a full skeletal cast of *Mamenchisaurus*, dinosaur footprints, and a cutaway model of a *Tyrannosaurus rex* leg, as well as a children's center with hands-on dinosaur games and learning materials. In addition to these traditional offerings, there is a computer-animated exhibit called, "Dinosaurs: A Journey Through Time." Five moving, roaring models—*Tyrannosaurus rex*, *Pachycephalosaurus*, *Stegosaurus*, *Triceratops*, and *Apatosaurus* travel the United States during much of the year. But the Pacific Science Center is their home base. Phone ahead for details.

200 Second Avenue
  North
Seattle, WA 98102
(206) 443-2001

Admission: Low fee

Facilities: Rest rooms, gift shop, food available, wheelchair accessible

BURKE MUSEUM

Featured on the four-part public television series "Dinosaurs," this museum has several prehistoric replicas on display, including a saber-toothed cat and three small, fleshed-out, meat-eating dinosaurs. *Allosaurus*, *Megalonyx*, and a giant ground sloth are also represented in excellent displays. But a great many more fossil resources are stored away, waiting for proper preparation and display. (See Curator's Corner.)

University of
 Washington
Mail Stop D.B.-10
Seattle, WA 98195
(206) 543-5590

Admission: Donation requested

Facilities: Rest rooms, gift shop, food available, wheelchair accessible

GINKGO PETRIFIED FOREST STATE PARK

Though it survived in Asia, the prehistoric ginkgo plant suffered extinction on the American continent. It was eventually reintroduced into several U.S. locations, but the fossilized remains of the ancient ginkgo and more than 200 other plant species are exhibited at this state park. Cut and polished samples of fifty species are on display in the park's interpretive center, but it is perhaps the "Trees of Stone," along a three-quarter-mile trail outside the center that best bring ancient history into modern focus. This locale dates back 15 to 20 million years.

P.O. Box 1203
Vantage, WA 98950
(509) 856-2700

Admission: Low fee

Facilities: Rest rooms, gift shop, wheelchair accessible

Megalonyx

THE DINO-TREKKING SITES 133

CURATOR'S CORNER

DR. J. M. RENSBERGER

Burke Museum
University of Washington

"I grew up in Miami, Florida," Dr. Rensberger remembers. "During my childhood, I lived a short distance from a veritable jungle of tropical trees that covered several city blocks and contained birds, snakes, and insects. This environment probably influenced my interest in animals.

"But the big moment in my early years happened when I was between five and six years old and accompanied my parents on a trip to the Smithsonian Institution in Washington, D.C. One of my clearest memories of childhood is the huge *Brontosaurus* skeleton. I remember being greatly impressed. It seemed to be composed of dark, stonelike bones that I knew must be very old. I also remember numerous glass cases with other spectacular fossils. I spent that entire day in the museum, until my parents had to carry me out.

"Two events combined to launch me into graduate studies of fossil vertebrates. The first occurred when I was sixteen, and visited Colorado. I climbed the 14,255-foot-high Longs Peak in Rocky Mountain National Park, and fell in with another climbing party—a group of geology students from MIT. I thought that being a geologist must be great if it involved climbing mountains. That was

how I came to study geology in college.

"The second event that propelled me into studying old bones was a single course that I took in 1955. During a field trip to a fire-clay quarry south of Boulder, we found a small slab of rock containing dinosaur footprints. Later in the spring, I took a roommate to the quarry and we collected more than a dozen dinosaur tracks for the geology museum at the university. Knowing how precious museums hold such specimens, I imagine they are still there.*

"I am still collecting museum specimens. When I came to the University of Washington, there were only about 400 fossil vertebrate specimens in the Burke Museum. We now have 45,000 curated specimens, rather equally distributed from the late Mesozoic to the Cenozoic. We are planning a new, permanent exhibit that will include a number of dinosaur specimens in addition to the *Allosaurus* we are currently showing."

*Author's note: Unfortunately, staff at the University of Colorado geology department "lost track" of Dr. Rensberger's tracks some time ago, most likely because they were collected prior to the construction of an "official" curated museum. If any readers know where these tracks wound up, we'd love to hear from you with the verifiable details.

WEST VIRGINIA

BLUESTONE MUSEUM

 This small local museum has a modest collection of local fossils and minerals to explore. A taxidermist is also on staff, so look also for exhibits of well-preserved wild animals native to West Virginia.

Summers County
 Chamber of Commerce
206 Temple Street
Hinton, WV 25951
(304) 466-1454

Admission: Low fee

Facilities: Rest rooms, wheelchair accessible

WEST VIRGINIA STATE MUSEUM

This is an all-around history museum, dedicated to West Virginia's most significant features. However, some natural history is included in the displays, including a selection of ancient amphibian tracks and a petrified tree trunk from an ancient West Virginia landscape.

Capitol Complex
Cultural Center
Charleston, WV 25305
(304) 558-0220, or
 (304) 558-0162

Admission: Donation requested

Facilities: Rest rooms, gift shop, wheelchair accessible

CURATOR'S CORNER

DR. GEORGE DEEMING

Curator
West Virginia State Museum

"West Virginia fossil geology dates to the Devonian, Mississippian, Pennsylvanian, and Pleistocene periods. The land that is now West Virginia was almost always covered by sea water," Dr. Deeming says.

"During the Devonian Period, plants colonized the earth, and flourished during the Mississippian and Pennsylvanian periods. Most of the great coal beds now found in West Virginia were laid down at this time.

"Picture a shallow, swampy inland sear, heavy with humidity and rich in insect and plant life. Amphibians splash and vocalize in their eagerness to feed. Their fossil remains can commonly be found in streambeds and mine discard dumps known as "tailings," throughout West Virginia.

"The West Virginia State Museum displays sections of fossilized *Lepoddodendrons*, *Lycopodia*, *Calamites*, *Cordaites*, and seed ferns. A large slab of shale displays the footprints of an unknown amphibian. Dioramas depict the period responsible for the geology of the state."

WISCONSIN

GEOLOGY MUSEUM

This museum's Ice Age elephants, called mastodons, were obviously not dinosaurs. They were mammals, now long extinct, with a fascinating fossil record in Wisconsin, where dinosaurs are rare. They are on display in skeletal form, along with such other Wisconsin native Ice Age mammals as *Glyptodon* (similar in appearance to an armadillo) and *Titanotheres* (a gigantic, rhino-like creature). Prehistoric marine fossils are also common in Wisconsin; this museum's eighteen-foot mosasaur is a good example. Thanks to the Black Hills Institute of Geological Research in South Dakota, the museum recently added a thirty-five-foot *Edmontosaurus* to its collection. In fact, the University of Wisconsin paleontological crew is currently hard at work excavating one of the finest *Tyrannosaurus rex* specimens ever discovered in Montana. (See Curator's Corner.)

University of
  Wisconsin-Madison
Lewis G. Weeks Hall
1215 West Dayton
  Street
Madison, WI 53706
(608) 262-2399

Admission: Low fee

Facilities: Rest rooms, gift shop, food available, wheelchair accessible

MILWAUKEE PUBLIC MUSEUM

Famous for creative exhibit designs, this museum didn't forget the dinosaur fan! "Dinosaurs" re-creates both the mysterious giants and their habitats, as seen by the vision of exhibit designers. Other exhibits, such as those on rain forests and ancient peoples, round out the museum. *Torosaurus*, *Triceratops*, *Pachycephalosaurus*, and *Tyrannosaurus rex* are represented in one way or another, as are Ice Age mammals, including samples of the first mastodon hair ever recovered. Call Milwaukee's tourism board at (800) 231-0903 in advance to see if Milwaulkee's annual "Dinosaur Days" fall during your scheduled vacation days.

800 West Wells
Milwaukee, WI 53233
(414) 278-2702

Admission: Low fee

Facilities: Rest rooms, gift shop, wheelchair accessible

ICE AGE INTERPRETIVE CENTER

 Some time after the dinosaurs suffered a mass extinction, mammals began to thrive. This educational center offers a look at those Ice Age creatures and the environment that contributed to their survival and, for some, caused their extinction. Not only are videos, photographs, and murals on hand for review, but an interpretive hike across the "Pothole Trail" will give you a firsthand look at just how an Ice Age glacier slipped across the landscape, leaving a torn-up path behind.

P.O. Box 703
St. Croix Falls, WI
 54024
(715) 483-3747

Admission: Low fee

Facilities: Rest rooms, gift shop, wheelchair accessible

CURATOR'S CORNER

DR. KLAUS W. WESTPHAL

Director
Geology Museum, University of Wisconsin

Although the Geology Museum has for many years possessed an impressive paleontological collection, like all good and ambitious geology museums, it longed for a dinosaur to call its own. Enter the Black Hills Institute of Geological Research, whose founder, Peter Larson, had discovered a quarry of *Edmontosaurus* near Rapid City, South Dakota. The Institute proposed that if Dr. Westphal, director of the University of Wisconsin's Geology Museum, could put together a team to assist in excavation of the duckbills, one complete skeleton would return to Wisconsin with the team.

It didn't take long to round up a group of expert and student paleontologists to accompany Peter Larson on his fossil quest. Those volunteers, along with crews from the Black Hills Institute, spent thousands of dollars and man-hours getting to the dig site and carefully separating dirt from dinosaur. But in the end, after three consecutive summers of grueling effort amid the dirt, snakes, and sweltering heat, the well-worn volunteers from the University of Wisconsin-Madison proudly brought home their ultimate treasure.

WYOMING

TATE MINERALOGICAL MUSEUM

After watching fossil resources trickle out of the state for lack of adequate federally sanctioned repositories in Wyoming, this small state college and its paleontologist Dr. Robert Bakker, with other experts, set out to build a fossil collection at the Tate Mineralogical Museum. They have gotten off to a strong start and plan to add more. In addition, the museum co-sponsors a yearly dinosaur conference, called "DinoFest," for fans of all ages. It has been held in mid-June, but call to be sure. It may be small now, but plans are mighty big!

Casper College
125 College Drive
Casper, WY 82601
(307) 268-2447, or
(307) 268-2514

Admission: Donation requested

Facilities: Rest rooms, gift shop, food available, wheelchair accessible

WYOMING STATE MUSEUM

Outstanding in this museum's paleo exhibit is an ancient bison skeleton and one solitary mammoth tooth found at a Wyoming kill site. In fact, the prehistoric exhibit is quite limited. But because dinosaurs are so much a part of Wyoming's history, officials book traveling dinosaur exhibits whenever possible.

Barret Building
Central Avenue
Cheyenne, WY 83001
(307) 777-7022

Admission: Low fee

Facilities: Rest rooms, gift shop, wheelchair accessible

DINOSAUR DIG

You can visit this fascinating dig site by calling the Cody Chamber of Commerce for directions and information on public displays. This dig itself, sponsored by the Smithsonian Institution, is an adults-only experience. If you are interested, you can make arrangements in advance with the Chamber of Commerce. But be prepared to pay a handsome fee to the Smithsonian. If you are willing to make that kind of investment, you'll find the expert guidance provided by the staff from the National Museum provides you with an amazing opportunity to learn firsthand how a dig really operates.

c/o Cody Chamber of Commerce
P.O. Box 2777
836 Sheridan
Cody, WY 82414
(307) 587-2297

Admission: High fee

Facilities: None

GREYBULL MUSEUM

This is a collection of fossils from what some experts have called "world-class dinosaur bone beds." Those beds are are actually located only a few miles east of this museum.

325 Greybull Street
Greybull, WY 82462
(307) 765-2444

Admission: Low fee

Facilities: Rest rooms, gift shop, wheelchair accessible

FOSSIL BUTTE NATIONAL MONUMENT

Fossils from a prehistoric subtropical lake highlight Fossil Butte National Monument. Not dinosaurs but ancient crocodiles, fish, birds, and even bats thrived in the humid setting fifty million years ago. Staff members, including a full-time park paleontologist, are eager to educate the public—especially kids—about the world's fossil resources. The visitor center provides several interesting exhibits as well as junior ranger hiking programs.

P.O. Box 592
Kemmerer, WY 83101
(307) 877- 4455

Admission: Low fee

Facilities: Rest rooms, gift shop, wheelchair accessible

UNIVERSITY OF WYOMING GEOLOGICAL MUSEUM

A full-sized copper model of a *Tyrannosaurus rex* stands just outside the main entrance of this museum, which, according to some, houses the state's best fossil collection, although the competition has been stiff in recent months. Included are an *Apatosaurus* skeleton, a *Triceratops* skull, and a juvenile *Maiasaura*.

P.O. Box 3006
Laramie, WY
  82071-3006
(307) 766-4218

Admission: Donation requested

Facilities: Rest rooms, gift shop, wheelchair accessible

BIGHORN CANYON VISITORS CENTER

Two dinosaur fossils are on display at this visitor center, but Pliocene mammals are the primary focus of this state-run facility. Don't miss the interpretive hiking trails, and if you tire of prehistoric animals, a wild horse preserve is only minutes away.

20 East Highway 14A
Lovell, WY 82431
(307) 548-2251

Admission: Low fee

Facilities: Rest rooms, gift shop, wheelchair accessible

CURATOR'S CORNER

RACHAEL BENTON

Staff Paleontologist/Ranger
Fossil Butte National Monument

"When you think of park rangers," says Ms. Benton, "you often think of someone with a shiny badge who answers kids' questions—someone on a first-name basis with Smokey the Bear. That's true, of course. But now there is a special type of ranger who not only takes care of trees and wildlife in our national parks, but also watches over fossils. I suppose you could call them 'fossil rangers.'

"Well, that's what I am—a ranger who takes care of fossils. Did you know that many of our national parks contain important fossils? Because they are within a national park, they belong to all of the people of the United States of America. Fossils are important resources that give us information about what our Earth used to be like, millions of years ago. They can tell us about climates of the past, and about how plants and animals have changed through time. But, just like wildlife, fossils need to be protected. If we allow fossils to be stolen or to erode away, we lose important information about Earth's history.

"How do we protect fossils on federal lands? Mostly, we start with the kids who visit the park. We try to show them how important fossils are, and explain why fossils need to be protected. There are lots of things that kids can do at fossil parks. Many parks have lots of neat fossils on exhibit, and sometimes there are people preparing fossils in a nearby prep lab. Park rangers offer special programs on how to identify different types of fossils. Some rangers show kids how to make casts or prepare fossils.

"Rangers also protect fossils by encouraging scientists to visit the parks and study the fossils found there. If fossils are not collected and studied, they will soon erode away. And finally, rangers keep a watchful eye over the fossils. It is illegal to collect fossils without special permission.

"I hope that you will take time in your travels to stop and visit a fossil park."

COMO BLUFF DIG SITE

 Paleo greats from Cope and Marsh to Colorado dinosaur expert Dr. Robert T. Bakker have frequented Como Bluff, searching for their life's greatest find. But the land is now private property, and amateur discovery is somewhat discouraged. Staff members at the wonderful Native American–focused Medicine Bow Museum will occasionally hand out written instructions for visitors to find the historic dinosaur locale, if they sense that the visitors can be trusted to respect both the owners of the land and the rare fossil resources just under the surface. More than twenty-six different species have been recovered from Como Bluff, and more are undoubtedly to come. Write or phone in advance for details.

c/o Medicine Bow Museum
P.O. Box 187
Medicine Bow, WY 83239
(307) 379-2383

Admission: Low fee (at the museum)

Facilities (museum only): Rest rooms, gift shop

WESTERN WYOMING COMMUNITY COLLEGE MUSEUM

Local residents speak in glowing terms about the new geology museum put together, in large part, by dinosaur enthusiast and curator Charles Love. Included are fossils native to Wyoming, as well as six full-size dinosaur replicas.

2500 College Drive
Rock Springs, WY 82901
(307) 382-1600

Admission: Donation requested

Facilities: Rest rooms, gift shop, wheelchair accessible

SHERIDAN COLLEGE GEOLOGY MUSEUM

Sauropod material recently excavated near Sheridan is one of the highlights of this small but growing local museum of geology, which also features a *Pachycephalosaurus*. Call ahead for up-to-the-minute exhibit information.

3059 Coffeen Avenue
Sheridan, WY 82801
(307) 674-6446

Admission: Donation requested

Facilities: Rest rooms, gift shop, wheelchair accessible

WYOMING DINOSAUR CENTER

P.O. Box 868
Thermopolis, WY
 80443
(307) 864-5522

Admission: Low fee

Facilities: Rest rooms, gift shop, wheelchair accessible

One of the most remarkable dinosaur stops listed in this book, the Wyoming Dinosaur Center offers not only an outstanding collection of dinosaur exhibits comprising more than ten complete skeletal mounts (*Triceratops*, *Allosaurus*, and a number of pterosaurs included), but also a working fossil lab. What makes the center truly unique, however, is the fact that it is located on more than 730 acres of rich Morrison and Cloverly formation bone beds. Every ten minutes an air-conditioned bus takes visitors from the museum to the actual bone beds where camarasaurs, stegosaurs, an allosaur, and Wyoming's first *Brachiosaurus* are being excavated by skilled paleontologists willing to answer questions as they work. Definitely not to be missed!

Triceratops

CANADA

ALBERTA

CALGARY ZOO, BOTANICAL GARDENS AND PREHISTORIC PARK

Although this is a traditional zoo, a collection of about twenty cement-form dinosaur and other prehistoric models from the Mesozoic Era are on display outdoors for fossil enthusiasts to enjoy.

P.O. Box 3036 Station B
Calgary, Alberta
 T2M 4R8
(403) 232-9300, or
 (800) 661-1678
 (Calgary Convention
 and Visitors Bureau)

Admission: Low fee

Facilities: Rest rooms, gift shop, food available, wheelchair accessible

ROYAL TYRRELL MUSEUM OF PALEONTOLOGY

Considered the ultimate dinosaur museum by those who should know, the Tyrrell features skeletal mounts from a dozen (or more) dinosaur species, including *Albertosaurus, Centrosaurus, Coelophysis, Corythosaurus, Dromaeosaurus, Hadrosaurus, Hypacrosaurus, Lambeosaurus, Ornitholestes, Sauronitholestes,* and *Tyrannosaurus.*

P.O. Box 7500
Drumheller, Alberta
 T0J 0Y0
(403) 823-7707, or
 (403) 823-7709

Admission: Low fee

Facilities: Rest rooms, gift shop, food available, wheelchair accessible

DRUMHELLER DINOSAUR COUNTRY

Rather than a specific dinosaur stop, this city is listed because of its all-around enthusiasm for anything prehistoric—inspired by a wealth of significant fossil finds in the area. Many local businesses have adopted saurian themes, including a dinosaur trail campground, a dinosaur trailer park, and much more. While in Drumheller for the Tyrrell Museum, don't miss the community fun!

c/o Big Country Tourist
 Association
P.O. Box 2308
Drumheller, Alberta
 T0J 0Y0
(403) 823-5885

PROVINCIAL MUSEUM OF ALBERTA

 Restoration models of *Ankylosaurus*, *Corythosaurus*, and *Struthiomimus*, and fossil specimens of *Lambeosaurus* are this museum's key features.

12845 102nd Avenue
Edmonton, Alberta
T5N 0M6
(403) 453-9100

Admission: Low fee

Facilities: Rest rooms, gift shop, wheelchair accessible

TRACK SITE (ANKYLOSAUR)

This track site was originally discovered by a Canadian oil company. Phone or write the Grand Cashe Chamber of Commerce for directions.

c/o Grand Cashe
   Chamber of Commerce
Grand Cashe, Alberta
(403) 827-3790

DINOSAUR PROVINCIAL PARK

One of the richest dig sites ever excavated, this Canadian treasure is unofficially overseen by paleontologist Phillip Currie (of the Royal Tyrrell Museum of Paleontology). Dinosaur models are also a part of the park experience.

P.O. Box 60
Patricia, Alberta
T0J 2K0
(403) 378-4595
   (Patricia Dinosaur
   Corner Services)

Admission: Low fee

Facilities: Rest rooms, gift shop, wheelchair accessible

TYRRELL MUSEUM FIELD STATION

Technically, this field station falls under the umbrella of Dinosaur Provincial Park, which opened in 1987. But this research center offers additional information, including fossil-preparation techniques and other educational programs.

P.O. Box 60
Patricia, Alberta
T0J 2K0
(403) 378-4342

Admission: Low fee

Facilities: Rest rooms, wheelchair accessible

BRITISH COLUMBIA

UNIVERSITY OF BRITISH COLUMBIA

 This university teaching museum has a good collection of fossil exhibits on display.

Geology Museum
Vancouver, British
 Columbia
(604) 822-5586

Admission: Free

Facilities: Rest rooms, food available, wheelchair accessible

NOVA SCOTIA

PARRSBORO NOVA SCOTIA

Several small gem and mineral shops and museums are sprinkled throughout Halifax, Nova Scotia—inspired by a wealth of Triassic and Jurassic bones regularly exposed by low tides. A call to the local department of tourism at the phone number listed will yeild a current listing, but included are the Geological Mineral and Gem Museum and the Parrsboro Rock and Mineral Shop, whose owner, Eldon George, boasts that he exhibits the world's smallest dinosaur footprint and calls his community "the dinosaur capital of the world."

Nova Scotia
 Department of
 Tourism
P.O. Box 130
Halifax, Nova Scotia
 B31 2M7
(800) 341-6096

Admission: Various fees

Facilities: Rest rooms

NOVA SCOTIA MUSEUM

For years, the people of Nova Scotia harbored some serious resentment against American fossil collectors—especially collectors from Harvard and Yale—because although they welcomed scientific discovery, they were somewhat annoyed that many of the fossil riches wound up on display in the United States. A small collection of those fossil finds have been returned and are on display in the Nova Scotia Museum today.

1747 Summer Street
Halifax, Nova Scotia
 B3H 3A6
(902) 429-4610

Admission: Low fee

Facilities: Rest rooms, gift shop, wheelchair accessible

ONTARIO

CANADIAN MUSEUM OF NATURE

Fossil specimens from *Anchiceratops*, *Daspletosaurus*, *Dromiceiomimus*, *Leptoceratops*, *Panoplosaurus*, *Styracosaurus*, and *Triceratops* are on display in the "Life Through the Ages" halls, which covers two floors. Also featured are marine reptiles and various multimedia educational aids to explain the life changes illustrated through exhibits and displays.

P.O. Box 3443,
  Station D
Ottawa, Ontario
  K1P 6P4
(613) 996-3102

Admission: Low Fee

Facilities: Rest rooms, gift shop, food available, wheelchair accessible

ROYAL ONTARIO MUSEUM

Another impressive Canadian museum, paleontologically speaking. *Albertosaurus*, *Allosaurus*, *Camptosaurus*, *Chasmosaurus*, *Corythosaurus*, *Edmontosaurus*, *Hadrosaurus*, *Lambeosaurus*, *Ornithomimus*, *Parasaurolophus*, and *Prosaurolophus* are exhibited, in one form or another.

Toronto, Ontario
  M5S 2C6
(416) 586-5549

Admission: Low fee

Facilities: Rest rooms, gift shop, food available, wheelchair accessible

QUEBEC

REDPATH MUSEUM

This is a smaller teaching museum, but the fossil collection is still worth seeing. *Majungatholus*, *Sauronithoides*, *Zephyrosaurus*, and parts of the oldest known reptile are on display. Also of interest is the fact that Redpath was the first Canadian structure built specifically as a museum, in 1882. Many exhibits are still displayed in a turn-of-the-century style to honor that sense of national history.

McGill University
859 Sherbrooke West
Montreal, Quebec
  H3A 2K6
(514) 398-4086

Admission: Low fee

Facilities: Rest rooms, gift shop, wheelchair accessible

SASKATCHEWAN

SASKATCHEWAN MUSEUM OF NATURAL HISTORY

"Megamunch," a robotic *T. rex* on display at the Saskatchewan Museum, stands as a silent symbol of the purchasing power of kids, because local students raised the money to create the exhibit. Although other earth-science exhibits are included at the museum, paleo resources include mosasaurs, dinosaurs such as *Edmontosaurus* and *Triceratops*, and early mammals such as mastodons and bone-crushing dogs.

College and Albert
  streets
Regina, Saskatchewan
  S4P 3V7
(306) 787-2815

Admission: Low fee

Facilities: Rest rooms, gift shop, wheelchair accessible

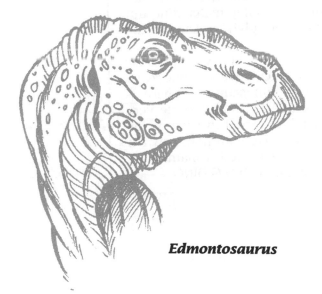

Edmontosaurus

TRAVELING DINOSAUR EXHIBITS

DINAMATION INTERNATIONAL

189A Technology
  Drive
Irvine, CA 92718
(714) 753-9630

Not only does Dinamation create magic for educational videos, television, and motion picture purposes—the company makes a lot of impressive dinosaur noise just for you. A series of its spectacular exhibits have crisscrossed the United States and the world since its start in 1980, stopping at museums, shopping malls, dinosaur parks—you name it. With well-known expert advisers, Dinamation makes every effort to remain on the cutting edge of paleontological theory both in dinosaur appearance and behavior. Because paleontological reconstruction is highly speculative—no one really knows for sure about many aspects of dinosaur life—there is bound to be some disagreement among experts. But some very respected scientists believe in the work reflected in Dinamation exhibits. Write for information about tours near your hometown or travel destination. And while you're at it, ask about Dinamation's special excavation opportunities by calling (800) DIG-DINO.

THE DINOSAURS OF JURASSIC PARK

The Dinosaur Society
200 Carleton Avenue
East Islip, New York
  11730
(516) 277-7855

You might have wondered, "What ever happened to the dinosaurs they used to make Steven Spielberg's *Jurassic Park*? Well, many of the dinosaur images you saw on the film were actually computer-generated animation. But there were models for some of the smaller dinosaurs, and those models as well as background sets are traveling the United States—and in fact the entire globe—to benefit the Dinosaur Society, a nonprofit organization dedicated to making accurate dinosaur information available to dinosaur fans. But the society is more than a dinosaur fan club. Any money raised in excess of expenses is awarded to real-life dinosaur research programs by way of grants. Thanks to the Dinosaur Society, award-winning paleontologists can continue their research, helping uncover not only dinosaur fossils, but the facts within those giant bones. For more information, see the Dinosaur Society entry under "Memberships/Clubs" in the Dino-Shopping Guide section of this book.

MR. BUDDY DAVIS

1040 Henpeck Road
Utica, OH 43080
(614) 668-3321

Most of Mr. Davis's forty-plus dinosaur models tour auditoriums and shopping malls in the northeastern and southern states. But plans for expansion are under way, including an educational program for elementary schools. Write for up-to-the-minute details and tour schedules.

KOKORO DINOSAURS

6005 Yolanda Avenue
Tarzana, California
  91356
(818) 996-8303

This Japanese company is considered key competition for Dinamation's touring robotic dinosaurs. Though different in some basic issues of style—Kokoro tends to include a great many more prehistoric mammals in its traveling exhibits—they are both excellent in their attention to detail, and similar in their basic exhibit designs. Write for details and tour schedules.

CURATOR'S CORNER

RAYANN HAVASY

Former Executive Director
The Dinosaur Society

"On June 11, at the American Museum of Natural History in New York City, an exhibition created by the Dinosaur Society made its debut. To this date, 'The Dinosaurs of Jurassic Park' remains the best-attended exhibition in the history of that museum, More than 600,000 people in New York alone will have the opportunity to see and learn about the science fact and movie fiction concerning these creatures from long ago.

"The Dinosaur Society, specifically Don Lessem, assisted Steven Spielberg in technical matters in the making of the movie *Jurassic Park*. In response, Steven Spielberg became an ardent supporter, even contributing to dinosaur science and research. His enthusiasm about dinosaurs prompted him to generously allow the Dinosaur Society to create his dinosaurs and design an experience that not only entertains but teaches.

"As people enter the exhibit, they see scenes, via monitor, from *Jurassic Park*, which prepare them for their experience in this 7,500-square-foot exhibition. They enter a world that people have never seen before."

PART TWO

YOUR DINO-SHOPPING GUIDE

WHERE TO FIND GREAT DINOSAUR STUFF!

BIRTHDAY PARTIES

ORIENTAL TRADING COMPANY, INC.

P.O. Box 2308
Omaha, NE 68103-2308
(800) 228-2269

(mail-order catalog)

Everything you could possibly need for a dinosaur birthday party—or virtually any party—is available at very reasonable prices through the Oriental Trading Company. Party favors, balloons, piñatas, pencils, erasers, confetti, stickers—anything you might need for a birthday or a class or club party. Dinosaurs are just the beginning. Ask for their $5 discount (with minimum purchase) on your first order.

Ichthyosaurus

CLOTHES

(See also Miscellaneous.)

SERENGETI

(free mail-order catalog)

This is definitely not a "dinosaurs only" catalog. In fact, only one of more than fifty shirts features dinosaurs. Wildlife of other kinds is highlighted in most designs. But the one dinosaur shirt offered—"They Ruled the Earth"—is outstanding.

P.O. Box 3349
Serengeti Park
Chelmsford, MA
 01824-0933
(800) 426-2852

AMERICAN MUSEUM OF NATURAL HISTORY

(gift shop)

Saying the American Museum has T-shirts sounds almost absurd. But in fact the American Museum has so many dinosaur products, it would take a catalog to describe them all. Not a bad idea, huh? Anyone at the American Museum listening? Write for details.

Central Park West at
 79th Street
New York, NY 10024

COMPUTER SOFTWARE

There is a flood of dinosaur-related software. Listed below are a few of our favorites, and a list of distributors and manufacturers who have dinosaur material waiting for your review. Apart from the two mentioned immediately below, beauty is in the eye of the beholder. Let the buyer beware!

DINOPARK TYCOON

DinoPark Tycoon is a really engrossing IBM-compatible computer game for virtually all ages. It's about the art of buying dinosaurs, dinosaur land, and dinosaur food, building dinosaur fencing, creating dinosaur advertising, hiring dinosaur-expert employees, running dinosaur gift shops—every detail down to cute little Tiki torches—and keeping it all together amid a grab bag of special conditions. Younger children might not grasp the complexities of running a dinosaur "business," but with a little adult assistance, children as young as three years old can enjoy the game. Older children will have you beat in no time, if you don't watch your screen. Best of all—it's even reasonably priced.

MECCA
6160 Summit Drive
  North
Minneapolis, MN
  55430-4003
(612) 569-1500

MICROSOFT DINOSAURS

(multimedia CD-ROM)

This is a remarkable collection of facts and illustrations. Narrated by dinosaur author Don Lessem, this effort effectively blends humor with accuracy, making it as interesting to children as to adults—as much fun for the dinosaur beginner as it is for the intermediate fan. Experts may find it "old news," but experts probably don't need instruction via a CD-ROM anyway. If you invest in only one dinosaur program for your multimedia computer system, Microsoft Dinosaurs would serve you well.

Other Dinosaur-linked Computer Companies:

1. Asymetrix *(Jurassic Park Screen Saver)*   (800) 370-8994

2. Byron Preiss Multimedia
   (The Ultimate Dinosaur)   (212) 645-9870

3. Creative Multimedia *(Dinosaur Safari)*   (503) 241-4351

4. Computer Support Corporation
   (Jurassic Art)   (214) 661-8690

5. Draw to Learn Associates
   (Draw to Learn—Dinosaur Edition)   (714) 263-0910

6. Knowledge Adventure
   (Dinosaur Adventure/Dinosaur 3D)   (818) 542-4200

7. Ocean of America *(Jurassic Park)*   (408) 954-0201

8. Revell-Monogram
   (Secret of the Dinosaurs)   (708) 966-2500

9. Sanctuary Woods
   (The Last Dinosaur Egg)   (415) 578-6340

10. Sony Electronic Publishing
    (Dinosaurs! Multimedia Encyclopedia)   (800) 326-9551

11. SoftBooks *(Jurassic Dinosaurs)*   (714) 586-1284

12. Westwind Media *(Dinosource)*   (800) 937-8555

Iguanodon

FINE ART

SCHEELE FINE ARTS

(mail-order catalog, $10.00)

Don't expect budget poster art from Scheele. Expect framable work from some of the finest paleo artists in the world, including John Gurche and Stephen Czerkas. If you want prehistoric-themed art you can be proud of, you won't be disappointed with Scheele.

P.O. Box 18869
Cleveland Heights, OH
   44118
(216) 421-0600

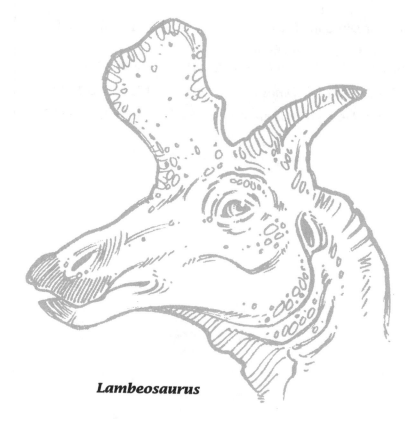

Lambeosaurus

FOSSILS

Whenever you consider purchasing authentic fossil materials, please take every precaution against buying illegally obtained paleontological treasures. Fossil theft robs future generations of their prehistoric legacy. But if a legal permitted collection can be documented, and you're willing to pay some very substantial fees, these organizations will be happy to hear from you.

BLACK HILLS INSTITUTE OF GEOLOGICAL RESEARCH

P.O. Box 643
Hill City, SD 57745
(605) 574-4289

The Black Hills Institute is the place for one-stop shopping, whether you're a private rock-hound or represent a museum. You'll find everything from small fossil and mineral collections to books and jewelry to toys and dinosaurs. The Larsen family and their associates work long hours to collect, prepare, and mount fossils for worldwide sale or donation and scientific study. Enthusiasts are welcome to watch as technicians prepare a wealth of fossil specimens ranging from the gigantic *T. rex* to the smallest ammonite. And you can always find something to bring home.

GREEN RIVER GEOLOGICAL LABS, INC.

365 North 600 West
Logan, UT 84321
(801) 750-0136

(free mail-order catalog)

Green River has fossil rights to a *Hadrosaurus* quarry, so dinosaur bones (from fragments to a complete skeleton) are for sale. But this organization actually specializes in collecting and selling prehistoric fossil fish. Specimens will cost you anywhere from $1 to thousands of dollars, depending on the rarity of the fossil. In addition to real fossils, casts are available.

PALEO SEARCH

P.O. Box 621
Hays, KS 67601

(mail-order catalog, $3.00)

Paleo Search is one of hundreds of fossil brokers—"middle men" who buy and sell fossils, most often collected by independent diggers. Most brokers do the best they can to ensure that collection has been done under legal conditions, but it is impossible to be sure. Paleo Search, however, believes their specimens are 100 percent legal.

THE STONE COMPANY

P.O. Box 18814
Boulder, CO 80308
(303) 581-0670

In recent years, the Stone Company has specialized in fossilized dinosaur eggs from Asia. The company has a great many fossil resources to offer the selective collector, however—most documented and quite expensive. Nevertheless, some fossil items are priced under fifty dollars and are worth consideration. Write for a catalog.

TRILOBITE TREASURES

P.O. Box 232 D
Thompson, CT 06277

(mail order)

Write for information on the purchase of a very common, legally obtained fossil that predates the dinosaur by millions of years. The trilobite, often called "the butterfly of the sea," is a delightful and interesting little fossil, within the reach and pocketbook limits of nearly all fossil enthusiasts. Many U.S. fossil museums and rock shops offer trilobites for sale, but if you can't find such an outlet in your area, check out what Trilobite Treasures has to offer.

Maiasaura

FOSSIL REPLICAS

(See also Miscellaneous)

DINO PRODUCTIONS

(free mail-order catalog)

This wonderful mail-order company specializes in all kinds of merchandise within the realm of natural history, including books, videotapes, posters, and toys. However, its fossil casts or copies are outstanding, and many are very inexpensive (under $10). Ask for their $5 discount (with minimum purchase) on your first order.

P.O. Box 3004
Englewood, CO 80155
(303) 741-1581

SKULLDUGGERY

(free mail-order catalog)

Skullduggery offers fossil casts—museum-quality copies of actual dinosaur and other prehistoric fossils. However, they are a little more expensive than Dino Productions merchandise—more appropriate for serious collectors than for eager kids. Skullduggery also sells dinosaur-related books, videos, fine art, and fossil kits.

624 South B Street
Tustin, CA 92680
1 (800) 3-FOSSIL, or
1 (800) 336-7745

JEWELRY

HORNY TOAD CONNECTION, INC.

(mail order/retail distributor)

9419 Central NE
Albuquerque, NM
  87123
(800) 880-9247, or
  (505) 299-9247

If you overlook this company's amazing little namesakes—sculpted into some of the most distinctive reptilian jewelry yet—you'll be missing a great conversation piece. But several dinosaurs are also featured in necklaces, earrings, and/or tie tacks. Ask for their free color brochure.

NATURE'S JEWELRY

(free mail-order catalog)

222 Mill Road
Chelmsford, MA
  01824-3692
(800) 333-3235

Dinosaur jewelry is hard to come by, but Nature's Jewelry usually offers at least one special dinosaurian piece, among hundreds of other styles (and some clothing).

VICTOR PORTER

P.O. Box 555
Windfall, IN 46076

Most of the jewelry listed in this shopping guide is costume jewelry. But Victor Porter is a master craftsman—who creates incredible, individual dinosaur art in the form of jewelry, for people who insist upon accuracy and attention to paleontological detail. His work is not inexpensive, but is worth every penny. If you want the best—for yourself or as a gift for the discerning dinosaur fan—Victor Porter is the man to write.

PM CREATIONS

(mail-order catalog, $3.00)

2648 East Workman
  Avenue
Suite 424
West Covina, CA 91791
(800) 392-9240

Included in PM Creations' catalog are six dinosaurian skull pins.

MEMBERSHIPS/CLUBS

DINAMATION INTERNATIONAL SOCIETY

Write for yearly membership fees and to find out what special offers go along with membership. Past premiums have included society membership pins, bumper stickers, and posters, as well as discounts on paleo classes and other merchandise.

P.O. Box 307
Fruita, CO 81521
(303) 858-7282

THE DINOSAUR SOCIETY

Founded by writer and dinosaur fan Don Lessem, the Dinosaur Society provides accurate dinosaur information to the general public. But a great many dinosaur experts enjoy membership in the Dinosaur Society. So this is a chance for ordinary dino fans to hear from authorities, by way of the quarterly newsletter (*The Dinosaur Report*) and Society merchandise catalogs. The Dinosaur Club offers younger fans a monthly newspaper (*The Dino Times*), a certificate, and a sticker. Fees vary; call for further information, and ask for a free copy of *The Dino Times*.

200 Carleton Avenue
East Islip, NY 11730
(516) 277-7855

THE DINO-TREKKING CLUB

Created for fun-loving dinosaur fans of all ages, our club offers a membership card, a bimonthly newsletter, special offers, and dinosaur discounts for a fee much lower than most other "clubs" currently in business. But unlike the others, ours is a nonprofit organization, dedicated to providing all dino fans with factual dinosaur materials—even if they can't afford the other memberships. A free four-month trial membership comes with the purchase of this book!

1042 15th Avenue
Longmont, CO 80501

THE DINO UNIVERSITY

505 Eighth Avenue
18th Floor
New York, NY 10018

This organization hopes to further the dino cause, via a unique person-to-person educational outreach called Dino University. A yearly membership fee ($29.95) covers membership benefits including a membership card, a dinosaur model, a poster, a puzzle, a marker, a ruler, and a free issue of its magazine, *Dinosaurus*. But one thing sets this program apart from other paleo clubs. Members can test their dino knowledge via specialized quizzes, graded and returned by Dino University experts.

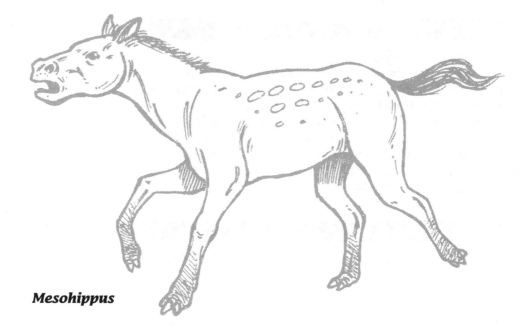

Mesohippus

MODELS/SCULPTURES

ANTS

This is not the place to find budget dinosaur models. Ants features only the best of dinosaur and other prehistoric models in the multi-hundred-dollar price range. But if you want quality reproduction miniatures, and are willing to pay the price, these are fine! Past selections (preconstructed or in kit form) have included *Allosaurus fragilis*, *Deinoychus antirrhopus* (an ancient horse), and a one-half-scale prehistoric man skull.

P.O. Box 9208
Albuquerque, NM
  87119-9208
(800) 642-9267

MONSTERS IN MOTION

(mail-order catalog, $3.00)

Models by Jurassic Park, Lunar, Menagerie Productions, and other companies are just a part of Monsters in Motion's standard merchandise; the majority of its products are models molded directly from science-fiction film props and characters.

6312 East Santa Ana
  Canyon Road, #351
Anaheim, CA 92807
(714) 281-3007

MONSTROSITIES

(mail-order catalog, $2.00)

Dinosaur and other natural-history products are available through Monstrosities. Included are dinosaur models, skeletons, bronzes, and much more.

P.O. Box 1024
North Baldwin, NY
  11510
(516) 378-1338

RICK C. SPEARS

Commercial artist and exhibit designer Rick C. Spears has prepared one-of-a-kind dinosaur-restoration models for private collectors and museums across the country. These are serious works of art. Mr. Spears will work with buyers to develop and create a model or exhibit to fit their individual needs. His work is exceptional. Just check out the "Dino-Identifier" section of this book for more than seventy masterful examples of his dinosaur-restoration illustrations.

615 University Circle
Athens, GA 30605
(706) 543-8374

TAMIYA AMERICA, INC.

2 Orion
Aliso Viejo, CA
  92656-4200
(714) 362-2240

This is not a mail-order company. If you phone or write, however, they can advise you on your nearest Tamiya dealer. And once you find the dealer, you'll discover some of the best, most accurate dinosaur diorama models on the market today. Relatively easy to construct, the four Tamiya kits (*T. rex*, *Triceratops*, *Parasaurolophus*, and *Chasmosaurus*) are sold separately, but fit together as a single scene. They range in price from twenty-five to just under forty dollars each.

Mosasaur

POSTERS

(See also Miscellaneous)

RICK'S MOVIE GRAPHICS

(free mail-order catalog)

So many movie posters are listed in this catalog it will take you a good hour to explore them all. Even so, much of what the company has to offer is not mentioned. A few dinosaur movies are featured, but call if your favorite is not.

P.O. Box 23709
Gainesville, FL
  32602-3209
(800) 252-0425

MOVIE DINOSAURS

Jerry Ohlinger's Movie Material Store tries to keep classic dinosaur posters and movie stills in stock. Call or write for a complete list of posters from movies with dinosaur themes.

Jerry Ohlinger's Movie
  Material Store
242 West 14th Street
New York, NY 10011
(212) 989-0869

Moropus

POSTAGE STAMPS

DINOSAUR STAMPS (FROM GUYANA)

Hans Tropicals
P.O. Box 32315
Baltimore, MD 21208

DINOSAURS!

Dinosaurs are a popular subject, and appear in postal stamps from all over the world. Anything from cartoon dinosaurs to incredibly detailed dinosaur art has been featured in stamps from the United States, South Korea, New Zealand, Japan, Australia, and more. These two stamp organizations can help you get started on a paleo postal set of your own. But don't overlook local stamp-collecting groups if you decide you want to collect. They can clue you in on stamp shows and sales scheduled in your area.

Official Stamp Agency
Cheyenne, WY
 82008-0001

Protoceratops

TRADING CARDS

DINOCARDZ

Dinocardz are educational and fun—perhaps one of the finest series of dinosaur collecting cards ever created. Artwork by some of the best talents in the dino-art business appears on the front of the cards, and very accurate statistics are printed on the back.

309 Fourth Avenue
San Francisco, CA
 94118
(800) BUY-DINO

Torosaurus

MISCELLANEOUS

BRAINSTORMS

8221 Kimball
Skokie, IL 60076
(800) 231-6000

(free mail-order catalog)

Dinosaurs aren't the only offering in the Brainstorms catalog. In fact, everything from innovative inventions to scientific learning tools to juggling videos are a part of the Brainstorm experience. But here are just a few of the dinosaurian offerings in a recent catalog:

Walking Dinosaur Kits

Dinosaur Skeleton Tie

Dinosaur T-shirt

The Great Dinosaur Hunt Video

Dinosaur and Fossil Experiment Kit

Dinosaur and Things Game

Dino Globe

Dinosaur Egg Soap

Dinosaur Posters

Dinosaur Figure Factory

Dinosaur Hat

Dinosaur Enamel Pins

Dinosaur Books

Dinosaur Inflatable

CALIFORNIA PACIFIC DESIGNS/STICKERS

P.O. Box 2660
Alameda, CA 94501
(510) 521-7914

Some of the finest dinosaur stickers are distributed by California Pacific Designs. These "puffy" stickers are amazingly accurate and great, great fun! Write for a dealer near you.

CREATIVE IMAGINATIONS, INC.

10879-B Portal Drive
Los Alamitos, CA
  90720
(714) 995-2266

This is not a mail-order company, so it may not be prepared for telephone inquiries. But it produces or distributes a number of excellent educational dinosaur toys worth seeking out, including "Dino Ball"—an inflatable globe marking regional dinosaur finds with corresponding pictures—and "Create-a-Scene" dinosaur stickers. Write to find out where you can buy Creative Imaginations dinosaur products in your area.

DINOSAUR MEDALLIONS

P.O. Box 32
Westbury, NY 11989

A set of five twelve-gauge brass medallions is offered by this company, including *Allosaurus*, *Apatosaurus*, *Stegosaurus*, *T. rex*, and *Triceratops*. Write for details and up-to-the-minute availability.

DINO PRODUCTIONS

P.O. Box 3004
Englewood, CO
  80155-3004
(303) 741-1587

(free mail-order catalog)

If you love dinosaurs, *really* love them, it's worth the long-distance call to get Dino Productions' wonderful catalog. All or most of its offerings are well-respected, accurate dinosaur products. But one of the most outstanding and affordable categories is fossil replicas. From a raptor claw (for under five dollars) to more dinosaur teeth than you can shake a stick at (in the same price range), to more extensive, more expensive selections, Dino Productions brings fossil ownership within reach, thanks to its wonderful "fakes." But the whole catalog is worth looking over—and over, and over and over. Other sciences are also featured in similar merchandise.

THE DINOSAUR SOCIETY CATALOG

200 Carleton Avenue
East Islip, NY 11730
(516) 277-7855

Carefully selected products, including books and note cards, are featured in this yearly dinosaur catalog. Write or phone for details.

EDUCATIONAL TOYS, INC.

(free mail-order catalog)

A wide variety of both dinosaur and other educationally centered toys is available through this catalog. Write or phone for a free copy.

P.O. Box 630685
Miami, FL 33163
(800) 554-5414,
    ext. 109

FOSSIL DUST GREETING CARDS

Specializing in authentic, scientifically accurate artwork, these note cards and stationery products do not feature dinosaur "cartoons," but reconstruction illustrations you would be proud to send to amateurs or experts. Write for a free sample and a very reasonable price list. Include a self-addressed, stamped envelope.

1042 15th Avenue
Longmont, CO 80501

JURASSIC PLAY SAND

Jurassic Play Sand is authentic sand formed during the days of the dinosaurs. This pure red sand, made up entirely of tiny, rounded red quartz crystals, is dust- and dirt-free—a selling point that health-conscious parents might find appealing. But it's the bright red color and smooth, silky quality of the sand that has kids excited. Write for details.

Salix
60 East 600 South
Salt Lake City, UT
    84111
(801) 531-8600

NATIONAL WILDLIFE NATURE GIFTS

(free mail-order catalog)

The only common thread tying merchandise in this catalog together is that a percentage of the profits are donated to the National Wildlife Federation. Some outstanding dinosaur merchandise is available, however, that we've yet to see turn up elsewhere. Included in recent catalogs were the following items:

Snap-Together Dinosaur Bone Puzzle

Dinosaur Shower Curtain

Baby's First Dino Set

Dinosaur T-shirt and Poster

National Wildlife
    Federation
1400 16th Street, N.W.
Washington, D.C.
    20036-2266
(800) 432-6564

NATURAL SCIENCE BOOKCLUB

3000 Cindel Drive
Delran, NJ 08370-0001

Write for details about the Fossil Hunter's Library.

SKYFLIGHT MOBILES/DINOSAUR MOBILES

P.O. Box 974, Dept. E
Woodinville, WA 98072
(800) 766-8005

(free mail-order catalog)

Skyflight is not a "dinosaur" company, but it does offer a very nice mobile featuring prehistoric creatures for a reasonable price.

Plateosaurus

PART THREE

A DINO-IDENTIFIER

WHO'S WHO AMONG DINOSAURS AND PREHISTORIC MAMMALS

When you come across a prehistoric creature you haven't heard of, turn to this section. It provides key details and an illustration for each animal mentioned in *Dino-Trekking.* Each entry mentions the age in which the animal was thought to have lived.

Albertosaurus
Late Cretaceous

A "small" (30-foot) tyran-nosaur. These creatures' arms, equipped with two fingers on each hand, were so short the animal couldn't even reach its own mouth. They were perhaps used to steady *Albertosaurus* when rising from a prone position. Found in North America (Alberta, Canada).

Allosaurus
Late Jurassic

Largest meat-eater of the Jurassic period, this animal averaged 30 feet long, but specimens have been found as long as 39 feet. Some experts say *Allosaurus* was quick and agile and hunted in packs to bring down large plant-eaters such as *Apatosaurus*. Others say they were clumsy and slow, and there-fore were scavengers that fed on "left-overs." Found in North America (Colorado, Utah, Wyoming), Africa, and Australia.

Amphicyon
Middle Oligocene to Early Miocene

This large 6-foot, 6-inch mammal resembled a bear with wolflike teeth. The bear-dog lived a life much like that of the modern grizzly bear. Found in North America (Nebraska) and Europe.

Anatosaurus
Late Cretaceous

An obsolete name for the duckbill now known as *Edmontosaurus* (see page 183).

Ankylosaurus
Early Cretaceous

The largest known ankylosaur, this armored dinosaur grew up to 33 feet long, weighed up to four tons, and was well protected by substantial armor. When attacked, the *Ankylosaurus* may have simply stood its ground, waiting for a chance to swing its heavy, spiked tail at the aggressor. It had a broad skull (almost two and a half feet wide), with two spikes sticking out of each cheek and two on each side of the back of its head. It also had a toothless beak. Found in North America (Alberta, Montana).

Apatosaurus
Late Jurassic

This creature's name means "long-necked lizard." Once called *Brontosaurus,* which means "thunder lizard," this 70-foot-long, 33-ton animal must have sounded like thunder when it moved, or, for that matter, breathed. *Brontosaurus* was actually the second name assigned this species, so science dictates use of the first name, *Apatosaurus.* This dinosaur, a sauropod, could rear up on its hind legs to fight off attack or reach the vegetation it fed on. Most experts believe it could also whip some meat-eaters into retreat with its massive tail. Found in North America (Colorado, Oklahoma, Utah, Wyoming).

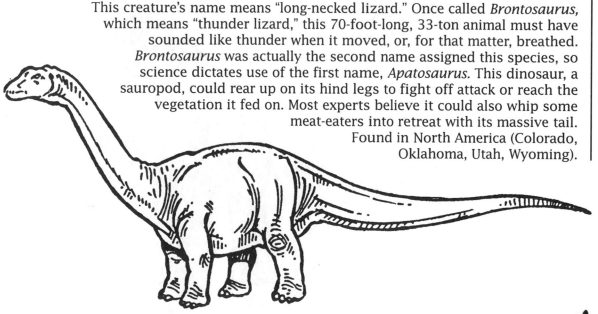

Archaeopteryx

Late Jurassic

This ancient bird, first found in Germany in 1861, is a classic in history. One of the earliest birds ever discovered, it had the signature "wishbone" configuration of collar-bones exclusive to birds, and feathers were found imprinted alongside bone in fossils. Some say these feathers were strictly for insulation, and *Archaeopteryx* could only glide. Modern theory, however, suggests it could fly, but not with the strong strokes of modern birds. It was about 24 inches long. Found in Europe.

Archelon

Late Cretaceous

Unlike the modern turtle, this enormous creature's shell was a framework of bone with a thick, rubbery skin stretched across it. It had paddle-like flippers for efficient swimming. It had no teeth, and its jaws apparently lacked strength, so it likely fed on jellyfish. Found in North America (Kansas, South Dakota).

Archidiskodon

Early Miocene to Early Pliocene

This is a primitive mastodon named for the Nebraska man who made the discovery. But it is likely a kind of *Gomphotherium* or an *Amebelodon,* based on reference materials considered reliable by the American Museum of Natural History in New York. About ten feet tall and found in North America (Colorado and Nebraska, although similar species were also found in Arizona and Florida), Europe, Asia, South America, and Africa.

Baluchitherium

Oligocene

Also (and more accurately) known as *Indricotherium,* at 26 feet long, this is the largest land mammal known to have lived. It weighed 33 tons and resembled a strange cross between a rhinoceros and a horse. It was elephantlike in many respects, such as leg structure, and it browsed on tree leaves with a unique arrangement of teeth—two upper teeth pointing downward, two bottom teeth jutting straight out. Found in Asia.

Barapasaurus

Early Jurassic

This is the world's oldest sauropod— a standard, long-necked, browsing dinosaur. It had spoon-shaped teeth for plant-eating, and was 49 feet long. Found in Asia (India).

Brachiosaurus

Late Jurassic

Brachiosaurus is the one of the tallest animals ever found with its skeleton complete. Larger sauropods have been found, but their skeletal remains were incomplete. The *Brachiosaurus*'s unique feature is that its front legs were longer than its rear legs. Like all sauropods, it had nasal openings just above the eyes. There is no way to know for certain whether these passages were for breathing, or whether the animal might have taken in air via a fleshy passage (like an elephant's trunk) that would not show up in the fossil record. In support of this theory, modern elephants also have nasal openings on the tops of their heads. "Brach" averaged 75 feet long, and weighed 40 tons. Found in Africa and North America (Colorado, Wyoming).

Brontosaurus

See *Apatosaurus,*
page 175.

Camarasaurus

Late Jurassic

Camarasaurus had spoonlike teeth that may have enabled it to eat a great variety of plant life. Smooth stones have also been found fossilized in the gut of the skeletal remains of *Camarasaurus,* leading scientists to speculate that, like many modern birds, this creature may have swallowed stones to aid in digestion. *Camarasaurus* skeletal fossils have been found up to 59 feet long. Found in North America (Colorado, Oklahoma, Utah, Wyoming).

Camptosaurus

Late Jurassic

A relative of *Iguanodon,* many *Camptosaurus* have been found in the Morrison Formation of the Western United States. Bony plates that separated air-breathing passages from eating areas enabled *Camptosaurus* to eat and breathe at the same time, allowing it to eat more often and more efficiently, without stopping to breathe. Its rear legs had three-toed hooves, and its shorter front legs had similar hoofs. Adults were 20 feet long. Found primarily in North America (Colorado, South Dakota, Utah, Wyoming), although one species has been recognized in England.

Centrosaurus

Late Cretaceous

Rather ordinary within the frilled version of horned dinosaurs, *Centrosaurus* had three horns, one at the snout and two shorter ones above the eyes. It stood 17 feet long and fed on plant life, like its famous cousin *Triceratops*. It is thought that *Centrosaurus* and other horned dinosaurs migrated in herds to meet the needs of their voracious appetites. Found in North America (Alberta, Montana).

Coelophysis

Late Triassic

One of more than 50 small meat-eaters documented thus far, *Coelophysis* was between 8 and 10 feet long, and stood on powerful hind legs. Thought to be a swift, cunning hunter, *Coelophysis* apparently traveled in large groups or packs. Mammals had evolved toward the end of the Triassic Period, and were likely a primary food source for this animal. Some fossil findings suggest that the adult *Coelophysis* might have fed on their own young, as well. Found in North America (New Mexico).

Corythosaurus

Late Cretaceous

Found exclusively in North America thus far, this lambeosaurine duckbill was thirty feet long, and had a saillike crest from its forehead to the rear of its skull. The size of the crest seemed to vary with the animal's age. The crest on *Corythosaurus* was hollow. There are different theories to explain this, including a nasal cooling system, a defensive sense of smell to detect predators, and a honking device to emit a warning signal, much like a foghorn. Found in North America (Alberta and Montana).

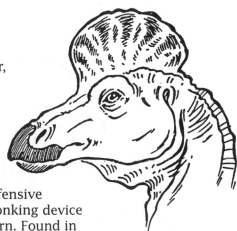

Deinonychus
Early Cretaceous

This deadly meat-eater was only 10 to 13 feet long, but was a streamlined, efficient hunter. Agile and quick, this intelligent carnivore had teeth with serrated edges (like all therapods) and could tear the flesh from its unlucky prey with ease. Named for a razor-sharp, sickle-like claw on the inside of each rear foot, it probably stood on one leg and kicked with the other. It is believed *Deinonychus* traveled and hunted in packs. Found in North America (Montana).

Dilophosaurus
Early Jurassic

Featured in Steven Spielberg's "Jurassic Park," *Dilophosaurus* did not have the frill or collar depicted in the film, and was considerably larger than its Hollywood cousin, at 20 feet long. A two-ridged crest has been found near the skulls of many *Dilophosaurus,* and supposition has determined the placement. But because not all fossils have the crest, some scientists believe it was a feature found only in males. Found in North America (Arizona, Connecticut).

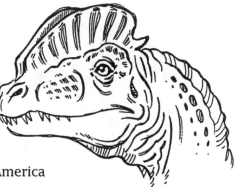

Dimetrodon
Early Permian

Known for the saillike ornamentation on its spine, *Dimetrodon* is an early reptile and, many believe, a likely ancestor to ancient and modern mammals. The sail is thought by some paleontologists to have been a temperature-control device. *Dimetrodon* was 10 feet long and probably weighed just over 400 pounds. Shearing teeth indicate that the *Dimetrodon* was a meat-eater, slow-moving until warmed by the sun. Found in North America (Oklahoma, Texas).

Dinohyus

Early to Late Miocene

This ten-foot-long mammal was built much like a pig or wild boar. The configuration of *Dinohyus* teeth indicate it could eat almost anything, and it is thought to have been an early scavenger. Found in North America (Nebraska, South Dakota).

Diplodocus

Late Jurassic

Almost 90 feet long, *Diplodocus* weighed only 11 tons. Both *Brachiosaurus* and *Apatosaurus* substantially outweighed it, but *Diplodocus* was longer than either of those sauropods. It probably reared up on its hind legs and stretched its 24-foot neck to reach the conifer branches it fed on, using its tail as a balancing third leg. *Allosaurus* and other allosaurs are thought to have been the only predator big enough to threaten *Diplodocus,* whose only defenses were to use its tail as a whip or rear up to crush the predator. Found in North America (Colorado, Montana, Utah, Wyoming).

Dire wolf

Pleistocene to recent

One of many species in the *Canis dirus* category. All domesticated dogs and nine living species of wolves, coyotes, and jackals originated with *Canis dirus*. Much like the modern wolf in appearance, this animal, six and a half feet long, was likely a scavenger rather than a hunter. California's Rancho La Brea has yielded remains of more than 2,000 dire wolves. Evidence collected there indicates that dire wolves and saber-toothed cats often battled fiercely. Found in North America (California).

A DINO-IDENTIFIER 181

Dirk-toothed cat

Late Miocene to Early Pleistocene

Megantereon, a saber-toothed cat, was often called "dirk-toothed cat," after the Scottish word for a dagger. Four feet long, it fed on larger grazing animals, and used the canines to down its larger prey. Found in South Africa, Asia (India), Europe (France), and North America (Texas).

Dryosaurus

Late Jurassic to Early Cretaceous

Thought to be swift and agile, owing to the nature and arrangement of leg muscles and tendons and the length of its shinbones, *Dryosaurus* was a herbivore well designed to evade predators. Its beaklike, toothless snout enabled it to clip the vegetation it fed on quite efficiently. Up to ten feet long, it stood on its hind legs while feeding and running. Found in North America (Colorado, Utah, Wyoming).

Dunkleosteus

Late Devonian

Of the placodermi class, this armored, jaw-less fish averaged 11 feet, 6 inches long. It was large enough and fierce enough to compete with ancient sharks for smaller prey. The body of *Dunkleosteus* was scaleless. Combined with an eellike tail, this provided *Dunkleosteus* with efficiency in swimming and hunting. Fanglike teeth at the front of its jaws gripped its victims, while cutting teeth behind sheared off sizable chunks. Found in Africa (Morocco), Europe (Belgium, Poland) and North America (California, Ohio, Pennsylvania, Tennessee).

Edmontosaurus

Late Cretaceous

Another hadrosaur or duckbill, *Edmontosaurus* had a toothless, beaklike snout with grinding teeth in rows behind. As in all dinosaurs, new teeth would replace aging or ground-down teeth. *Edmontosaurus* had as many as 1,300 teeth at one time. Feeding on coarse vegetation, such as pine needles, the teeth were capable of shredding. *Edmontosaurus* was quite large, averaging 30 feet long. Found in North America (Alberta and Montana).

Elasmosaurus

Late Cretaceous

This massive marine animal, 46 feet long, was the longest of the elasmosaur family, one of the longest plesiosaurs on record. More than half of its length was its neck, which was greatly flexible from side to side, but not so in vertical movement. Paleontologists suspect the animal paddled below the water, with its head clearly above water, most likely for better visibility, when "fishing." Once prey was spotted, *Elasmosaurus* dove after it head first. Found in Asia (Japan) and North America (Kansas).

Epigaulus hatcheri

Miocene

The only known horned rodent ever found, this mammal resembled a marmot, except for the two sharp horns above its nose and below its eyes. Some suggest it was ferocious, though it was primarily vegetarian. It may also have fed on insects. The horns are thought to have been ornamental, for mating purposes. It was one foot long. Found in North America (Great Basin region).

Eryops

Late Carboniferous to Early Permian

This early amphibian averaged 6 feet 6 inches in length and had bony plates along its spine, likely to support a bulky body on land. Because of its weight and its sluggish rate of movement on land, it very likely fed in the water. Found in North America (New Mexico, Oklahoma, Texas).

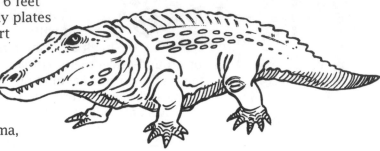

Glyptodon(ts)

Early Miocene, Pliocene, and Pleistocene

The mammalian version of ankylosaurs: armored giants much like the modern armadillo. They survived by grazing on grasslands, and existed recently enough to be included in Patagonian Indian legends. Reaching amazing sizes at times, one Pleistocene *Glyptodon* specimen found in Argentina was the size of a small automobile (five feet tall, ten feet long). Fifty genera have been found in South America and southernmost North America.

Ground sloth

Pliocene to Pleistocene

Many giant ground sloths on display in North American museums are *Glossotherium.* Recovered from California's Rancho La Brea tar pits, this massive mammal walked on its knuckles in an apelike fashion. It could rear up on its hind feet to reach the boughs it dined on. It was, on average, 13 feet long.

Hadrosaurus

Late Cretaceous

This was the first dinosaur skeleton found in North America (in 1858, by Professor Joseph Leidy). One of the hadrosauridae, the family of duckbills, *Hadrosaurus* was a biped and stood on its strong rear legs. Thirty feet long, it had no crest, but did have a pronounced bony bump on its snout. The "bill" of the duckbill had no teeth; the food was pulverized by a collection of teeth located at the rear of the jaw, in a vertical motion. Found in North America (Montana, New Jersey, New Mexico, South Dakota).

Haplocanthosaurus

Late Jurassic

This 60-foot-long dinosaur helped correct the early misconception that sauropods were crocodilelike animals, dragging their bulky, ten-ton bodies along the ground. Found in North America (the Morrison Foundation of Colorado).

Ichthyosaurus

Early Jurassic to Early Cretaceous

Part of the Ichthyosauridae family of "fish lizards," this marine dinosaur fed on fish, and resembled a fish, but it had no gills. Fossil finds in Germany produced adult animals with embryonic specimens preserved within the body cavity, suggesting that *Ichthyosaurus* bore its young live, in the sea, as modern sea mammals do. Like modern whales, *Ichthyosaurus* had to surface in order to breathe. Fossil remains from *Ichthyosaurus* have been found, with pigment cells that indicate that it had smooth, thick, reddish brown skin. It was up to sixty feet long. Found in Europe (England, Germany) Greenland and North America (Alberta, Nevada).

Iguanodon

Early Cretaceous

The second dinosaur discovered (1822), it was found even before the word *dinosaur* was coined, and mistaken initially for a large, rhino-like mammal. But the British physician Gideon Mantell knew its teeth were reptilian. Because they resembled those of the iguana of South and Central America, he dubbed the animal *Iguanodon* in 1825. After Mantell died, *Iguanodon* was incorrectly assembled in a four-legged stance. It was corrected in 1877 when Belgian mine workers discovered articulated skeletons. *Iguanodon* fed on ferns and horsetails, browsing on all fours. But it stood on its rear legs to reach higher plant life. About 30 feet long, *Iguanodon* has been found in Europe (England, Belgium, Germany) and North America (South Dakota).

Kritosaurus

Late Cretaceous

This 30-foot-long duckbill had only a slight bump, just below the eyes, rather than a crest, as seen in some other hadrosaurs. Many paleontologists believe *Kritosaurus* and *Hadrosaurus* are different species of the same animal, as they have this bump and other characteristics in common. What purpose the bump served is unknown, but speculation includes a sexual display among males only, or a defensive "bumper" for battles meant to determine which male will be dominant in the herd, or control a harem of females. Found in North America (Alberta, Montana, New Mexico).

Kronosaurus

Early Cretaceous

Though throughout much of prehistory, Australia was dry land, in the Early Cretaceous it was a shallow, warm sea, teeming with sea life. The largest pliosaur yet found (42 feet long), this massive creature had a skull nine feet long, significantly larger than that of the greatest carnivorous dinosaur, *Tyrannosaurus rex*. Found in Australia (Queensland).

Lambeosaurus

Late Cretaceous

Distinguished by its oddly shaped crest, this duckbill is believed to have been nearly 30 feet long, although one specimen found in California and thought to be a *Lambeosaurus* was 54 feet long. Information on the animal is still scarce. Possibly found in North America (Baja California, Montana, Saskatchewan).

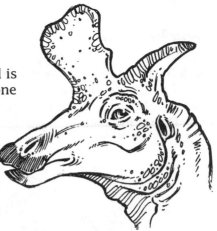

Latimeria chalumnae

The name means "living fossil," and this fish is so labeled because it was of a family believed to be extinct (Coelacanthidae) until one was netted in the waters dividing Madagascar and Africa in 1938. Species within the coelacanth family date back 380 million years.

Maiasaura

Late Cretaceous

Thought to be social animals, the "good mother" apparently laid her eggs with care, in a circular pattern, within craterlike nest sites. Layers of decomposing vegetation kept the eggs warm. Some scientists theorize that the hatchlings were "cute," with oversized eyes and tiny bodies, perhaps making them more attractive to the parents responsible for their survival. Adults were 30 feet long. Found in North America (Montana).

Mamenchisaurus

Late Jurassic

The neck of this gigantic animal made up almost half of its total length, which averaged 72 feet. As a result, the sauropod browsed among the tenderest top branches of conifers. Found in Asia.

Mammoth

Pleistocene

Different versions of the mammoth existed through-out the Pleistocene. Some species survived the Ice Age only to die out a short time afterward, perhaps hunted to extinction by early man. They differ from their early relatives, the mastodons, pri-marily in the structure and function of their teeth, and in their eating habits. They ranged from 9 to 15 feet tall, and have been found in Europe, Asia, and North America (South Carolina, Georgia, Louisiana, Florida, Nebraska, Maine).

Mastodon

Late Miocene to Late Pleistocene

This elephantlike mammal was related to the mammoth (see above).

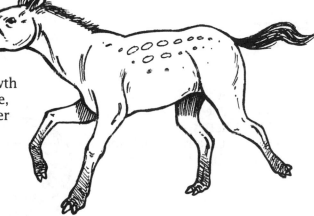

Megalonyx
Pleistocene

President Thomas Jefferson is credited with discovering this large North American ground sloth in West Virginia in 1797. Jefferson, an amateur paleontologist himself, called the creature Megalonyx—"large-clawed beast"—because of the enormous claws on the third digits of the hind feet. It has also been found in Alaska as well as in some Canadian provinces.

Mesohippus
Middle Oligocene

Early horses the size of greyhounds, these mammals were among the first to enjoy the freedom of open lands, rather than hiding in undergrowth or protection. Unlike the modern horse, *Mesohippus* had a three-toed foot rather than a hoof. Found in North America.

Monoclonius
Late Cretaceous

Bone fragments discovered in 1876 by the pioneering paleontologist Edward Drinker Cope were identified as being those of *Monoclonius,* a single-horned ceratopsian. Little has been found, however, other than bone fragments, from which to reconstruct the animals. Some paleontologists believe it resembled *Centrosaurus,* while others maintain they were one and the same. (See Centrosaurus, page 179.)

Moropus

Early to Middle Miocene

Something of a mystery animal, *Moropus* has been compared to a horse, a bear, and a rhino. But it seems to be something altogether different. Although it has no known modern counterpart, it was quite successful in its day, thought to have survived for 50 million years. Ten feet long, it had three-clawed toes, able to bend and manipulate tree branches to get at leaves, or to dig up roots, both of which scientists believe *Moropus* fed on. Found in North America.

Mosasaur

Late Cretaceous

Marine lizards thought to be distant relatives of the monitor lizard, these animals were well adapted to life within the warm waters offshore. Some types averaged about 15 feet, while others were quite large at 33 feet. It likely ate fish and other small and abundant sea life.

Moschops

Late Permian

The thickness of this creature's skull suggests it may have engaged in head-butting, not unlike goats or sheep. But this 16-foot-long animal was a massive reptile hardly resembling anything in a petting zoo. Its stocky forelegs were set wider than its longer rear legs. A herbivore, *Moschops* was sometimes prey to its meat-eating relative, *Titanosuchus.* Found in South Africa.

Nodosaurus

Late Cretaceous

This heavily armored, 18-foot-long animal had strong hips and legs to bear the burden of its protective ankylosaur armor. But its head was small and narrow, its plant-eating teeth inefficient. Found in North America (Kansas, Wyoming).

Ornithomimus

Late Cretaceous

Probably capable of running up to 30 miles per hour, this relatively small carnivorous dinosaur (about 11 feet 6 inches long) used its speed to evade the angry species whose nests it raided in search of food. But it is thought to have been omnivorous, in fact, with a diet that included leaves, fruit, insects, and smaller animals. It is often called the "ostrich dinosaur" because it resembles the flightless bird in many ways. Found in North America (Colorado, Montana).

Pachycephalosaurus

Late Cretaceous

Named for the unique dome of bone on its head (*Pachycephalosaurus* means "thick-headed lizard"), this animal was the largest of its kind. Its bony head was probably used for butting. It was a plant-eater, averaging 15 feet long. Found in North America (Alberta).

Parasaurolophus

Late Cretaceous

Another duckbill found exclusively in North America (Alberta, New Mexico, Utah), *Parasaurolophus* was 33 feet long, with a distinctive crest protruding from its skull. Scientists once believed the hollow crest was a sort of snorkel that allowed the animal to breathe while it fed underwater. Most now suspect, however, that the crest was used as a resonator for vocalization.

Peccary

Oligocene, Pliocene, and Late Pleistocene

Also known as tayassuids, these animals are related to modern pigs, although ancient versions were larger and, like today's wild pigs, often fierce. They had five toes on each foot, while modern pigs have two. It looked much like a meat-eater because of its protruding canine teeth, but it was a herbivore. Found in North America (Great Plains) and South America.

Pentaceratops

Late Cretaceous

Five horny structures were excavated with this 25-foot-long ceratopsid, hence the name *Pentaceratops.* But only three of the fossil horns represented true horns. Two were above the eyes, the third on the snout. The remaining two were part of its facial structure, and protruded from the cheeks, underneath the neck frill. Like its many cousins, *Pentaceratops* was a gentle plant-eater, though it was probably fierce when defending territory or its young. Found in North America (New Mexico).

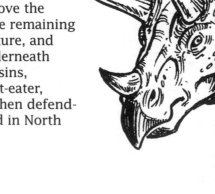

Phytosaur

Late Triassic

Phytosaur is a broad term for a number of crocodile-like amphibious carnivores. One common phytosaur—*Rutiodon*—had an average length of ten feet, as is about average among these animals. Various fossilized phytosaurs have been found in Europe (Germany, Switzerland) and North America (Arizona, New Mexico, North Carolina, Texas).

Plateosaurus

Late Triassic

This large prosauropod (a term meaning "before sauropods") and his very similar cousins throughout the world offer support for the theory that all landmasses were once connected. Though the 20-plus-foot-long herbivore was found in Europe (France, Germany, and Switzerland), very similar specimens have been found in China (*Lufengosaurus,* 20 feet long) and South America (*Coloradia,* 13 feet long). Although mass gravesites have been discovered, it is not known whether they lived in herds or simply died and were washed away to a common area.

Plesiosaur

Early Jurassic to Late Cretaceous

A general term for a group of early long-necked marine reptiles, 7 feet to nearly 50 feet in length, with paddlelike flippers. Many people imagine that the mysterious animal said to dwell in Scotland's Loch Ness is a plesiosaur, though scientists consider it highly unlikely. Most died out at the close of the Jurassic era. However, *Elasmosaurus,* found in Asia (Japan) and North America (Kansas) flourished until the very end of the Cretaceous period.

A DINO-IDENTIFIER 193

Protoceratops

Late Cretaceous

The famed paleontologist Roy Chapman Andrews brought back a number of *Protoceratops* fossils and fossilized eggs from his 1920s expedition to the Gobi Desert. Averaging 6 feet long and 400 pounds, this plant-eater had a neck frill and a beaklike snout. Found in Asia (Mongolia).

Pteranodon

Late Cretaceous

One of the largest of flying reptiles or pterosaurs, as they are commonly called, *Pteranodon* was probably a glider, with an average wingspan of 23 feet. It was toothless and probably fed on smaller fish, not unlike a pelican, swallowing them whole. The toothless feature was unusual, in that most pterosaurs had teeth. Found in Europe (England) and North America (Kansas).

Pterodactyl

Late Jurassic to Cretaceous

A general term for the pterodactyloidae suborder of pterosaurs. Some of the smallest known flying reptiles belong to this suborder (*Pterodactylus*, 2 feet 5 inches), as well as some of the largest (*Quetzalcoatlus*, 39 feet). Found in North America (Kansas, Texas).

Quetzalcoatlus

Late Cretaceous

Most flying reptiles have been discovered in ancient marine settings. This creature of massive wingspan (up to 39 feet) was found in Texas, and apparently lived far inland. Findings are not complete, but this appears to have been the largest flying animal of all time. It seems to have been a scavenger like the modern vulture, soaring high above the land, searching for abandoned dinosaur carcasses.

Stegosaurus

Late Jurassic

Adopted as the Colorado state fossil, *Stegosaurus* has been found in great abundance, relatively speaking, in that state as well as in Oklahoma, Utah, and Wyoming. Although a number of theories exist concerning how the arrowhead-shaped plates were affixed to *Stegosaurus,* certainty is impossible, since no fossil remains have been found with the plates still intact. Placement is arranged based on those theories. The inefficient teeth found in fossilized skulls suggest that *Stegosaurus* may have eaten only soft plants. They averaged 20 feet long, but specimens have been found up to 30 feet in length.

Stupendemys

Early Pliocene

This early freshwater turtle became extinct approximately 3 million years ago. It was the largest freshwater turtle of its time, at over six feet. Its closest modern relative is only 2 feet 6 inches long. It fed on weeds, and apparently could remain underwater for long periods to forage. Found in South America (Venezuela).

Supersaurus

Mid-Jurassic to Early Cretaceous

Found in Colorado in the 1970s, this relative of *Diplodocus* was enormous. Thought to be the largest of the Brachiosauridae (along with *Ultrasaurus*) until 1986, when *Seismosaurus* was found in New Mexico, measuring 130 feet long. After careful study, these temporary names may be updated, based on more detailed information.

Tenontosaurus

Early Cretaceous

Large compared with others in its group, *Tenontosaurus* was 30 feet long, and weighed about one ton. It resembled an iguanodont. *Tenontosaurus* had clawed feet for defense and foraging, but was likely no match for smaller, more ferocious predators such as *Deinonychus*.

Titanotheres

Eocene and Oligocene

A common term for members of the family Brontotheriidae, a group of rhino-like mammals. Some evolved massive horns, some did not. But the horns were actually bony structures covered with thick skin, unlike modern rhinos, whose horns are composed of compacted hair. Most were around eight feet tall at the shoulder. Found in Asia and North America.

Torosaurus

Late Cretaceous

The "bull lizard" was the last of its kind, and one of the largest, at 25 feet long. It is believed to have traveled in herds, much like the modern elephant, together with other, similar horned dinosaurs. Though it was a herbivore, few predators would have taken on the nine-ton beast; bulk alone would have been a great defense, and with its substantial horns, *Torosaurus* could have done battle with the best of challengers. Found in North America (Montana, Saskatchewan, South Dakota, Texas, Utah, Wyoming).

Triceratops

Late Cretaceous

Triceratops weighed in at an average of six tons, outbulking even the modern elephant, and was 30 feeet long. It was one of the most abundant dinosaurs ever found, and traveled in herds. Many well-preserved *Triceratops* have been found, thanks in large part to the massive structure of their skulls. Although Othniel C. Marsh found and named the first *Triceratops* in 1889, a second famous American paleontologist, Barnham Brown, was said to have seen as many as 500 *Triceratops* skulls in the field. Found in North America (Alberta, Colorado, Montana, Saskatchewan, South Dakota, Wyoming).

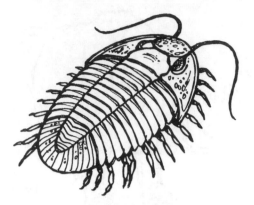

Trilobites
Cambrian to Late Carboniferous

Often called "butterflies of the sea," these small, jointed creatures were incredibly abundant. The largest known specimen, on display at the Smithsonian's National Museum of Natural History in Washington, D.C., was found near Dayton, Ohio.

Tyrannosaurus rex
Late Cretaceous

Perhaps the best known of carnivorous dinosaurs, *T. rex* has been called "the most terrifying engine of destruction ever to walk the earth." Measuring as much as 40 feet long and up to 15 feet tall when rearing up, this eight-ton beast's only real challenge was extinction. Though *T. rex* bones were found in the United States in 1902, a complete skeleton was not discovered until the late 1980s.

That specimen was promptly confiscated by the FBI in a dispute over legal ownership. Many believe the duckbill or hadrosaur was the primary food source for *Tyrannosaurus rex*.

Ultrasaurus

A sauropod relative of Brachiosaurus (see *Supersaurus,* page 196).

Xiphactinus
Cretaceous

Competitive with sharks of its time, *Xiphactinus* as long as 13 feet have been discovered. Some believe it fed on smaller specimens of its own kind, along with other fish. The modern "bony-tongued" fish are said to be related to these ancient hunters. Found in Europe.

Zygorhiza
Late Eocene

Though this is considered an early whale, it had a long, eel-like body. It did have other traits in common with modern whales: *Zygorhiza's* body was six times the size of its head, and it had the same seven vertebrae found in today's whales. But *Zygorhiza* had a short neck and ferocious, razor-like teeth not common to its modern cousins. Found in North America (Atlantic and Gulf coasts).

INDEX

Escalante Petrified Forest (Utah), 123

F

Fernback Museum of Natural History (Ga.), 34

Field Museum of Natural History (Ill.), 41, 44

fine art, 156

Flintstone's Bedrock City (S.D.), 109

Fort Worth Museum of Science & History, 118, 122

Fossil Butte National Monument (Wyo.), 139

Fossil Dust Greeting Cards, 170

fossils, 11, 17
  at Black Hills Institute, 112
  at Calvert Cliffs Park, 61
  at Doss Ranch, 122
  in Florida, 30, 33
  in Georgia, 34
  in Hagerman beds, 40
  in Mississippi, 69
  in New York State, 89
  preservation of, 52
  rangers for, 140
  replicas, 159
  shopping guide, 157-58
  in Virginia, 131
  in West Virginia, 135
  See also paleontology; *specific species and sites*

G

Garden Park Paleontological Society, 18

Geology Museum (Wis.), 136, 137

Ginkgo Petrified Forest State Park (Wash.), 133

Glyptodon, 114, 184

Grand Canyon Caverns, 7

Green River Geological Labs, Inc., 157

ground sloth, 52, 184

H

Hadrosaurus, 185, 186

Hagerman Fossil Beds National Monument (Idaho), 39, 40

Haplocanthosaurus, 185

Horny Toad Connection, Inc., 160

Hot Springs (S.D.), 109

Houston Natural Science Museum, 119

I

Ichthyosaurus, 79, 152, 185

Iguanodon, 155, 186

Illinois State Museum, 43

Indiana University–Purdue University Museum, 45

Indricotherium. See Baluchitherium

Iowa Historical Museum, 48

J

Jerry Ohlinger's Movie Material Store, 165

jewelry, 160

John Day Fossil Bed National Monument (Ore.), 102–3

Jurassic Park (movie), 6, 38, 149, 150

Jurassic Play Sand, 170

Jurupa Mountain Cultural Center (Cal.), 15

K

Kimmswick site (Mo.), 72

Kingman Museum of Natural History (Mich.), 65, 66

Knott's Berry Farm (Cal.), 13